HOME IN TIME FOR BREAKFAST

A First World War Diary

HOME IN TIME FOR BREAKFAST
A First World War Diary

Stuart Chapman

ATHENA PRESS
LONDON

ISBN 10-digit: 1 84748 008 X
ISBN 13-digit: 978 1 84748 008 8

First Published 2007 by
ATHENA PRESS
Queen's House, 2 Holly Road
Twickenham TW1 4EG
United Kingdom

Printed for Athena Press

In Loving Memory of my father, who died on 11 February 1967. Compiled by his daughter, Margaret Chapman.

With grateful thanks to Lieutenant Colonel W A H Townend MA of the Royal Artillery Historical Society for his considerable help with the research. Thanks also to Pauline and John for their encouragement.

My mother

The Great War, England 1916

Diary of events from my enlistment on April 26th

After a great deal of trouble I managed to get into the Royal Garrison Artillery (RGA).

Entrained at Charing Cross station at 11.15 a.m. on 26th April for Dover, where I arrived at 3 p m. We immediately had dinner then walked up the hill and reported at the barracks – Fort Burgoyne.

April 28th

I was vaccinated today and joined the signallers, as they were asking for volunteers. Shifted to the Duke of York's school about a mile distant from where I was inoculated. The first injection made me feel very bad but after an hour or so I felt better.

May 15th

Left Dover at 6 a.m. and arrived at Pembroke Dock at 9 p.m. the same day.

May 19th

Was weighed. 10 st 9 lbs.

May 20th

Second dose of inoculation.

May 24th

On cookhouse fatigue all day.

May 27th

Isolated for nine days as measles broke out in the tent.

June 6th

Finished our term of isolation. Moved from a tent into barracks.

June 12th

Commenced training for signalling.

June 30th

Went home for the weekend.

July 3rd

Returned from leave.

July 20th

Was put through electrical examination.

July 24th

Preliminary examination on everything.

July 26th

Passed out as first class signaller – 597.5 marks out of a total of 600.

July 28th

Going on six days' overseas leave.

August 4th

Had a service on the square in commemoration of the start of the War.

August 10th

We were given 24 hours notice to pack up and depart for Winchester.

August 12th

Arrived at Winchester and joined 175th Heavy Battery.

September 2nd

Leaving for Larkhill at 10 a.m. to go through a course of firing.

September 3rd

Arrived after a long march of 31 hours at 5 p.m.

September 7th

Battery commenced firing today. Finished firing course with full honours from the General.

September 8th

Going on six days' leave. Remainder of battery marching to Borden – a three-mile tramp.

September 13th

Due back from leave. Caught the 9.15 p.m. train from Waterloo. Arrived at Borden at midnight and had to park on the floor without any blankets and all our clothes on. Didn't get a wink of sleep.

September 19th

Names up in order for going to the front. Going sick with rash on my face.

September 29th

Off to France at 4 a.m. after an hour's jolly hard graft hauling guns on trucks in the dark. What a job it was getting the horses into the trucks. With some, we had to tie their legs to pull them in. We left at 5 a.m., arriving at Southampton at 8.30 a.m. Embarked for Le Havre on the *City of Dunkirk* at 5 p.m., after hanging about all day in the docks. Could not move away. Saw the *Aquitania* being loaded with coal.

Somme, 1916

September 30th

Arrived Le Havre at 11.30 a.m. Two ships had been sunk in the Channel, one by a mine and one by a submarine.

October 2nd

Admitted to 39 General Hospital, Le Havre. The 175th Battery is moving up country.

October 13th

Discharged from hospital. I was in for 13 days. Going to Honfleur, the RGA base details.

October 16th

Put in for a pass and had a good look around Le Havre, about seven miles away. The evening was very enjoyable.

October 23rd

Was detailed off to proceed up the line and join 37th Siege Battery, 3rd Corps, 27 Group. Left Honfleur at 6.15 p.m.

October 24th

Arrived Rouen at 7 a.m. Stopped in a YMCA until 2.30 p.m. and then entrained for an unknown journey. Was exchanging bully for apples with French corps on the road.

October 25th

Arrived Albert at 6 p.m. Total train journey was 29 hours. Walked to a village called Dernancourt about seven kilometres distant. Left there the same evening and rode in a waggon to another village called Lahoussoye, 14 miles away. Slept in a barn all night. At Dernancourt a shell dropped within 150 yards of the train – my first experience of them. I thought I was in for a good time. Some parts of Albert were in ruins, especially the station. I viewed the church with its overhanging spire. Three hours before we arrived at Dernancourt a shell had dropped right through the Heavy Artillery headquarters. They were clearing away the debris. None of our men were killed or injured but a great deal of damage was done.

October 26th

Left Lahoussoye in motors for Fricourt Circus. Walked from there to High Wood on the Somme about five miles. Arrived at destination at 7 p.m. There were guns and shells all around us firing day and night; it was just like hell. Wonder if ever I shall be able to endure the continual noise. The shell holes seem almost to be touching one another. It would not do for anyone to wander about in the dark as they would very easily break their leg or get drowned in large holes of water, etc.

October 28th

All night the sky was illuminated with the explosion of shells, liquid fire, rockets and fire balls from aeroplanes and trenches.

November 1st

Fritz is sending over plenty of shells.

November 3rd

Aeroplanes busy overhead – one of ours down.

November 4th

On gun detachment.

November 5th

A big strafing. All our guns synchronising and infantry going over the top.

November 6th

On detachment.

November 7th

A shell dropped within 20 yards of our dugout. We all had to fly with our steel helmets. Two of our officers were badly wounded with a grenade, which was accidentally kicked. The ground around here is simply alive with them; all covered with a thin layer of earth. At the least knock, off they go. The grenades were left as Jerry had to evacuate these trenches in a hurry only two weeks ago. One of the fellows who came with me to this particular battery was wounded by a splinter from a shell.

November 9th

Went to Bazentin Wood about four miles away to get rations for the battery. Watched a fight right overhead, which was rather exciting.

November 10th

Walked to Bazentin to carry home some iron girders.

November 11th

Helped to dig a new dugout for the officers.

November 12th

Went to Bazentin again and carried ordinance stores home, which was eight miles there and back. This was after we had pushed two trucks back to High Wood.

November 13th

A bombardment woke us up at 5 a.m. In was quite a cannonade and you could hear the trench mortars firing from our trenches three miles away. It is now 8.30 a.m. and not a gun can be heard anywhere. This morning I was helping to make a new officers' mess. Mounted guard at 3 p.m. for twenty-four hours. We had no guard room as a shelter but used the shed of No. 1 gun. Am now writing by the light of a candle, which is on the top of a shell. While doing my turn of sentry-go from 10 p.m. until 3 a.m. our picket lamp went out. It is our duty to see that it is continually burning during the night so I had the unpleasant job of relighting it. To anyone not accustomed to these trenches and shell holes etc., it is rather a gruesome task, especially when there is no moon. To walk to this light we had the use of an electric torch if it was very dark. On one journey we had to walk on a narrow raised railway line four or five feet from the ground and if we had missed our footing it was probable that we would have fallen and broken our legs, or simply have fallen in one of the many pits of water. It is not very hard to fall into great pits of water or mud and if one shouted for help it would be a long time coming, if it ever did, as it was almost suicidal venturing out after dark. I have seen myself go only a few yards away at night and lose my bearings and it would take a good while to get back.

November 14th

Finished guard at 3 p.m. A lot of German aeroplanes are hovering over us now. After tea, a counter-attack commenced.

November 15th

We are still digging a new officers' mess. We have been doing this now for two weeks. In the afternoon we all paraded at 1 p.m. and marched to Bazentin where our shells were dumped. Loaded up twelve bogeys and five or six men pushed each truck back to the battery. Then after we unloaded them we pushed all the empties back to the dump in High Wood – two miles away.

November 16th

It is very cold today, so much so that we have to break the ice out of the shell pits. The food is very poor. Have not had a dry foot for over two weeks. Every night I wash the mud out of my socks, which are usually saturated. All the mud is quite hard with the frost and it is a treat to be able to pick out dry steps. A shell landed not far from our Sergeant Major. He had a splinter right through his coat and escaped with only a fright. We were all ordered to move higher up out of the danger zone.

November 17th

Started at 9 a.m. for Bazentin. Unloaded trucks of 160 shells. Placed them on bogeys and pushed them home, arriving at 2.45 p.m. Was an extremely cold day. Felt very hungry for dinner, which consisted of stewed bully. We then took trucks back to the dump and on coming back saw an awful sight. About six bodies all heaped on a truck, all mangled by shells and some parts were hanging. It made one almost feel faint to look at them. Our 5 o'clock meal consisted of a little tea and nothing at all to eat. Only had bread and cheese for breakfast. We had a good day's hard work on starvation rations. Felt as if I could have eaten a horse. Saw a French aeroplane brought down today only a few yards from the battery; the machine was all smashed. On going to Bazentin yesterday I saw some infantrymen dig up one of our chaps by accident. He was placed in a waterproof sheet and they were going to bury him just as I left. The smell was unbearable. Evidently, when he was killed there was no time to dig a grave so, like many more under these circumstances; just a thin layer of earth was put over him. He had no head so expect it had been blown off. I met a fellow who came with me from the base in Honfleur but he branched off at Dernancourt to another battery. He had been sent home wounded but is now with another unit – so he was very unlucky. Have been to Bazentin to get shells again, the same routine as yesterday but two journeys instead of one. The whole day it poured and I was soaked through. For two miles or more on the Contalmaison Road I saw streaks of blood, apparently from the wounded going to the dressing station. It made me feel quite sick to see such a long trail and the snow being on the ground made it look very conspicuous. One of our officers was helping to push the trucks, which is very hard work when they are loaded with shells and all uphill. He remarked, 'You fellows earn your shilling a day'. Had a new pair of boots a fortnight ago and another today. It is proof of what continual mud will do to our footwear. They are too large and have made one foot quite sore and it is very painful to walk but the suction of the mud is partly the cause of it.

November 19th

On shell fatigue again. Finished at 12.15 p.m. In the afternoon I visited Bazentin and collected some wood for our dugout fire. Today I have had the smallest dinner ever since being in the army; one small tin of pork and beans between two people. There was none of the former and only two tablespoonfuls of beans; also a little cold tea. Our first meal was a third of a loaf each and cheese. At 4 p.m. we had a small drop of tea, two dog biscuits and butter and jam – the latter being a luxury. At night I find it hard to sleep, as I feel so ravenous. There is hardly a day that we could say all our food today would make one meal. The vermin at night also adds greatly to my restlessness. Sometimes I awake feeling very irritable. Yesterday I was soaked through to the skin and had to sleep with all my clothes on to dry them. Whilst in bed last night I was looking forward to my breakfast and my parcel, and longing for a piece of home-made cake. Sometimes I feel so hungry that I smoke a few cigarettes and it helps to take away that longing feeling.

November 20th

Again working on the officers' mess. Have taken all the chattels out of the old mess, half of the roof fell through and buried all the floorboards. I should think between 2–3 tons of dirt fell down. The officer in charge happened to see it falling and shouted out, otherwise some of the fellows might have been buried as they were underneath and only a yard away. This old mess was condemned on account of the smell of the dead bodies. It was built on the side of an old German trench. The ground here is extremely dangerous because it is infested with buried hand grenades. In addition, the smell of dead bodies is just about as much as one can bear. It is a wonder there is so little disease about.

November 21st

A new officer has come to our section and it appears that he has risen from the ranks, as one of the fellows here knew him when he was a sergeant in his battery. Had a fairly good night's sleep and for a change the vermin seemed to be quite agreeable. There are a number of chaps here going to hospital with influenza, rheumatics, etc.

November 22nd

Went to Bazentin Wood to get some fuel and on the road home I almost got lost, as it was so foggy. I sat down by the side of a grave to have a rest and my thoughts went to the fellow underneath. After arriving back I tramped to the divisional canteen, six miles there and back, to try and buy some candles. Being sold out, I proceeded to another camp a couple of miles further on. Passed Mametz Wood, but it was all in vain: someone had been there before me. It was a long walk home in the dark, empty handed. Felt fairly exhausted and could hardly put one foot before another. Altogether, it was twelve miles for nothing. The roads are in a shocking state for walking and my heel being raw made it a painful journey. On passing Bazentin I saw two 12 in. howitzers and one 15 in. on rails. The former were firing as I passed but they did not make much noise and not as much as our own. The latter is a huge gun and rarely fires unless in a bombardment.

November 23rd

Was on fatigue carrying bags of stones to place under our gun. After she has fired a few rounds she sinks right down in the mud. I was coming home and carrying some tins of water and fell down twice in the mud – right up to my knees. The more I wriggled the deeper I went down. Have seen a horse in difficulties and I could hardly pull him out. It took hours of hard work. Have seen carts sunk so low they have had to be left. If we were to have two days and nights of incessant rain it would be almost impossible for man or beast to move. The mud is terrible now, in fact it is heartbreaking to try and get about and puts years on one's life. Any little spirit that is left in one is almost lost. The shells are nothing in comparison to the everlasting torture of lice and the loathsome mud. To see me trudging along one would take me for an old man of sixty. Sometimes I have to rest after every hundred yards.

A busy day for Jerry. He was firing heavily and brought down some of our aeroplanes. Also a French one within 400 yards of us. They took two airmen away on stretchers. Didn't sleep again last night as I had a big attack of lice. Have been round collecting all the tins of bully I could find in the old disused trenches. Managed to find four tins and I have just eaten a whole one of 12 oz. Sometimes we come across scores of them and they are a great find when one is hungry. One of the chaps here is a real Christian. He thinks nothing of giving away all and going without himself and he often goes about looking for anything he can pick up. Last night while in bed Jerry sent over two large shells. We could hear them whistling and the report of the explosion was tremendous. Thought every minute would be our last and it made my heart feel as if it was in my mouth. It is the whistle that makes one feel that way because we cannot tell where it is going to drop but the report of the explosion sounded quite near. At night it makes one feel quite nervous of them yet we can only stop where we are and trust in God. During the day one can go further afield if it is getting too warm. At night it is different as you could easily run into danger and if one is going to be killed one might as well be in the company of others. Every morning when I awake I thank God we have been spared another night. The roof of our dugout would take between a five or six ton weight but if a medium or large size shell struck it it would be instant death. We would know nothing about it. The roof would stop a small shell and is splinter-proof. Every night I pray to God to save our souls and afterwards I feel quite contented. It is a grand thing to think we can get satisfaction and at least temporary contentment from prayer, especially under such adverse circumstances. I know that the Almighty will do all in his power to save us. If the worst should happen, I would die happy in the company of my comrades. Even at the most dangerous times my faith never falters in the power of God for it is He alone that controls our destiny. If ever we feel hungry or are short of anything the good Samaritan of ours always says 'Never mind, the Lord always provides' – a very nice proverb. It seemed to be very true, something always turned up even at the last moment. I should think our friend was a man with great faith. He never appeared to be afraid, was always self-sacrificing and going about doing all the good he could and always had a kind word and wore what I call a sincere smile. How a man like this is looked up to, even if it is only for consolement, and how few and far between they are.

November 24th

Had a wash down to the waist in a shell hole. Although this is forbidden it made me feel quite fresh and had the effect of a good bath. Five of our airmen were brought down yesterday and one of ours brought down a Jerry. Went to Bazentin again to get some wood for the cooks, once before and once after dinner. About 9 a.m. a corporal of the Royal Munster Fusiliers came to our dugout and asked if he could stay, as he felt sick and could barely move with the flu. He slept soundly until 2 p.m. He had some Oxo and coffee but could not eat anything. He went away thanking us for our hospitality and wished us luck. I always pity these infantrymen, poor chaps, as I feel they should have more preferences than anyone. He told us they have been without a rum issue for a week and they had to wait a long time for letters and parcels, especially the latter. A very quiet day for firing. A minute ago not a sound could be heard. Our menu today was breakfast: bread and cheese with tea; dinner: stew and tea, dripping and toast, cheese, pastry, cake, two kinds of biscuits, chocolate, mince pies, pasties, coffee and almonds, etc. Quite an assortment.

November 25th

Have been water carrying for the cooks and peeling potatoes. The weather is very miserable. It has been raining all day and the water and mud about is too awful for words; in fact this is the greatest enemy we have to contend with. The vermin were so abundant last night that I slept without a shirt. Although I had a bit of a bath yesterday it has made practically no difference. My boots and puttees were so wet that I had to sleep with the former on all night as I should never be able to get my boots on in the morning and having a sore heel makes it more awkward. Was on detachment today. My boots and puttees were saturated with mud from yesterday. In the afternoon I walked to Bazentin to unload a truck full of shells – between 400 and 500. Also 25 boxes of cartridges and 20 boxes of fuses. It has stopped raining now, yet still very muddy.

November 27th

Took off my steel waistcoat because it makes it easier for me to sleep and a great relief as I can feel free to ease the constant irritation. Paraded at 8 a.m. to go to Bazentin to load up eight trucks of ammunition that had been brought here by motor. Fritz is shelling very heavily near the battery; his aeroplanes are also very busy.

November 28th

Was on detachment in the morning and went to Bazentin to bring away eatables from the CO's motor car. Collected some fuel at the wood for our own use. At 5.30 p.m. I was called out to help unload three truckloads of shells.

November 29th

All day helping the 19th Heavys – the 19th Heavy Artillery Battery – the next battery to us. We were assisting them to pull three guns out of the mud. These are long range and rather heavy guns. There were between forty and fifty men pulling ropes. Some of our fellows were helping them all day yesterday and only moved the gun between five and six yards. This battery is shifting to a quiet part of the line for a rest. One of our officers was injured by a grenade and had to have his legs amputated. He is said to be disfigured for life and is a very nice fellow by all accounts. One of our boys was taken to hospital with trench feet. Today it is bitterly cold and handling that cold rope makes it more so.

November 30th

On detachment today. I often hear the bagpiper playing in the distance; the infantry are evidently being relieved. Having my dinner by the side of the gun while Fritz is sending over shrapnel. We are helping the ammunition party to unload the shells. Have done practically nothing all day, only hanging about in the cold. My feet this morning felt frozen but since I have had dinner they are much warmer. On shell fatigue – brought up six loads. On the way to the battery we had to take every shell off by hand and tip the trucks over so as to let some wounded go by who were also on trucks. What a system! Only one single line – this is an everyday occurrence. I call it disgraceful. Fellows might die going to the dressing station. Fancy them having to wait fifteen minutes or more every now and again while someone emptied their loads so as to let them go by. A great many have died on the way and the sights outside these dressing stations reminds one of a graveyard.

Took empty trucks back and went to Bazentin for another load. Twelve men were detailed to take the empties back but I was lucky enough to get out of it. That always seems to be a load on a burden after two journeys of shell carrying. The 17th Heavys have just taken all their guns and other articles away. Two chaps out of this dugout have shifted to new quarters and wanted us to follow. I am not superstitious but have got so used to this old place that I don't want to leave it. It has a good strong roof and it would take a direct hit to bury us. There are only two of us here now. Fritz has been shelling heavily round here tonight. Had a letter from a friend of mine that I left behind at Borden – we both joined up together at Dover. Was on detachment today and very busy firing. Were over at the old 17th Heavys' quarters looking round for anything we could get hold of. We were digging a recess for cartridges. Was prevented from sleeping last night although I only changed clothes yesterday. This afternoon I boiled all my clothes for three hours. Hung some out today and am letting them stop out for a few nights so as to get frozen. There was supposed to be a gas attack last night; some were warned about it and some were not. The attack came off about six in the evening.

December 4th

Was on detachment until teatime and fired 17 rounds. This is the first bright day for a week but very cold. In this week's 'Answers', I read that the Kaiser was a prisoner in one of his own castles in Germany and was placed there by the Crown Prince. It was said that the Kaiser's last attack was not an illness at all. He was mobbed by his own people and got hurt.

December 5th

Was on fatigue making a new guard room. Another fellow and myself went over to the 17th Heavys and took all the sandbags we could get for our own use. Have this moment received 20 francs pay; the first I have had in this battery and only the second since I have been in this country. Fritz sent over a shell that exploded 300 yards in front of our battery. It hit a gun shed of the RFA. No one was killed but three were injured. I saw one of the injured being taken away on a stretcher with his head bandaged and he looked very white. It is proposed that our Major is giving us 100 francs for the Christmas festival.

December 6th

On detachment in the morning and in the afternoon was enlarging a dugout.

December 7th

In the morning twelve of us carried a bag of mail each to a place called Ehen, 27th HAG headquarters near Manetri Wood, five miles distant. In the afternoon we had to fill in two refuse holes near the cookhouse. The MO made a complaint about the smell. Weather very misty and mild.

December 8th

Mounted guard at 3 p.m. A canteen is being made for us and we had to light the picket lamp three or four times last night. If we see the SOS signal – two red and two green – we have to give the detachment warning. The rest of the battery were called out at 9.30 last night to walk to the Contalmaison Road to carry home some officer's kit and it is extremely muddy. It was fortunate for me that I was on guard as I missed it. Today it has been constantly raining. There are rivers of water everywhere. After tea I went twice to the tank to get some water. It was pouring with rain and each time I nearly fell into a pool of mud. We are supposed to go out in twos to light the picket lamp because if one was to meet with an accident on the road the other would be able to go for help.

December 10th

Paraded at 2 p.m. for shell fatigue. Brought back one load after waiting two hours.

December 11th

Went to Bazentin at 8.30 a.m. for rations. Brought up one full trolley load including yesterday's mail. On the way there Jerry sent over a shell, which dropped not more than 30 yards from us. We all fell flat. I looked round and could see the mud and slush rise up 100 or more feet high. It seemed nearly on top of us. There was an artillery man killed along this road the other day by a splinter of a shell. One is liable to be killed within 500 yards of where the shell bursts.

December 12th

Took mail bags to 27th HAG at Ehen. On returning had a feed at the canteen. Arrived back about noon and remained there the rest of the day. Today it is extremely cold and we have had a heavy fall of snow.

December 13th

Taking mail bags again today. Coming home we saw a large tree being blown up with dynamite. It was a tremendous upheaval and roots and dirt flew everywhere. Thought to myself, *what a mess that would make of me!* This weather is very bad for my feet. I have never felt fit since being here and at times it is a hard job for me to crawl along. It makes me feel languid and like an old man. A fellow said to me that it is a wonder how we all stand these uncouth surroundings. He himself could hardly get along with his rheumatism but would not give in. His was a bad case and could easily have been admitted to hospital. Yesterday's tramp made me practically soaked with mud. One fellow was covered up to the waist in mud and had to sleep in his clothes and wear them the next day. There is no chance of having a bath and one's feet become black with the continual soaks. Can you wonder that the troops do not feel fit? To add greatly to my discomfort is the cumbersome steel waistcoat. It is simply torture wearing it every day. Many is the time I have felt like throwing it away but have kept up my spirits and seemed to hear someone say to me, 'The day you discard that you will surely be hit'. Out here our boots and puttees do not wear out – they rot. Had a new pair only two weeks ago and now another. Every day I wash all the mud out of my socks but the puttees are clogged with it.

December 14th

Felt very cold in bed last night and could not seem to get warm. Found it difficult to get up and when I did I felt rather queer. Did not have any breakfast as the sight of bread of cheese made me feel sick. Feel all shivery as if I have a touch of flu. Walked to Bazentin to take away a load of Xmas stuff for the officers' mess. Had another journey in the afternoon. I went to bed at 6 p.m., not having had anything to eat all day.

December 15th

Received four large parcels from Mother. This morning I feel much better yet still a little weak. Was carrying water for the cooks. Gave my clothes a good washing with Keatings.

December 16th

Collected two bags of bricks for the trail of our gun and on returning was told that I was promoted to head chef so I immediately reported myself to the cookhouse. Was very busy all day and am delighted with the change as there are heaps to eat. Am only here while another chap is away on leave. I commence duties at 6.30 a.m. and finish at 4.30 p.m. My first job in the morning is lighting the fire.

December 17th

Had two more parcels from home.

December 20th

Some of our chaps are going to Bazentin today. Came across a fellow with the back part of his head off. He had just been hit and was lying in a pool of blood. It was a ghastly sight. The Sergeant Major read out an order about the bad habit of using water outside the dugouts. The shell holes have been old latrines, are infested with dysentery and enteric germs and must on no account be used. Further, anyone not using whale oil every night and who has trench feet will get all leave stopped for the battery. I started using it for my feet and believe it has kept the cold out all day.

December 21st

Another fourteen men have gone on leave today from this battery. Was issued with a fur coat. Firing is very quiet today on both sides. While I was chopping up wood, a piece flew up and hit me on the nose and I was stunned for a few seconds. It was a nasty cut.

December 22nd

Have heard that Germany will accept any of our peace terms. We all hope it is right and are a little jubilant over it.

December 23rd

Two Indians came down here today and asked us if we would boil them a dixy of water. One seemed quite happy. He was singing away to himself and it sounded quite funny. When he had his water he was given some tea and was delighted, exclaiming '*trés bon*' and clapping the cook on the back.

December 24th

Managed to get a shirt out of the store, the only one to my name. The others are torn to threads and this is not much better. Very busy in cookhouse today, getting prepared for tomorrow's feast. Having Xmas and Boxing Day's rations in today.

December 25th

We fired over 200 rounds yesterday between 8 a.m. and 2 p.m. For dinner we are having fried steak, sprouts, greens and potatoes, quarter of a pound of Xmas pudding, custard and figs, walnuts and oranges. The Sergeant Major came down in the morning slightly inebriated and asked if everything was all right. Each man could have a pint of beer and a tot of rum. We were all more than satisfied. A lot of shells – 300 – came up and we gave Fritz the compliments of the season. It is very quiet just now, not a sound can be heard, just like Sunday afternoon at home. Am writing this on my own in the dugout, sitting by the fire and every now and again stopping to put a little wood on.

December 26th

Some of our fellows were drunk. One fell in a shell hole and it was very dark. This was midnight and he was only a few yards from his shelter but it took him nearly an hour to find it. Battery firing hard all day, giving it hot to Jerry now. There were more aeroplanes up yesterday than I have ever seen and plenty of fights in the air.

December 27th

Returned to duty today. Was in the cookhouse twelve days all together. Came out about 10.30 a.m. intending to do a good day's washing etc., but was warned for guard duty at 1 p.m. Here I am in a portable guard room at 6 p.m. and I go on first turn from 7 p.m. until 9 p.m.

December 28th

Last night Fritz was sending shells over very heavily, which were landing on the road just near the dugout. A terrific report was heard in the early morning: it was a shell dump exploding at the back of our battery due to being shelled itself. Going to shift my quarters tomorrow as it is somewhat lonely here. There are four men in this new place and will be good company. There were twelve here; the remainder are in hospital with severe colds. One went away today for the second time – an extremely nice chap. Very superior and quite a gentleman, but not very strong. Only this minute I have lit the siege lamp and in the event of action going I am to place it on the gun ready to show a light for setting the sights. Last night I was scratching myself to pieces and doing the same this morning. The Corporal had evidently noticed me at it and told me to go away and have a good hunt. I changed my clothes, which were simply swarming. It is heartbreaking to have to endure it all. One sometimes feels as if one would go mad with the irritation. Left off the steel waistcoat and feel sure that it harbours the lice. All alone now. The other fellow went on guard at 3 p.m. as I came off. Two of us went to light the lamp last night and got lost and it took us the best part of an hour to find our way back.

December 29th

Carrying water for the cooks. Have just settled down to new quarters. They are all bunks and appear to be nice and comfy.

December 30th

On fatigue taking up a small railway used for bringing up shells to the guns on trucks. We carried them to the battery. On ration carrying in the morning and the afternoon on detachment. Slept down section dugout all night. Saw one of our boys carried away on a stretcher. He was wounded in the back by shrapnel while on guard and I believe he was shortly to go on leave.

December 31st

Called away at 8.30 to go to Bazentin for shells. Have taken one and a half loads to the battery and am looking after the remaining half load – 72 shells – in a siding while the engine comes back from the battery. The slush that is about now is terrible. No one would credit it unless they saw it for themselves. The place for miles is nothing more than a sea of mud and I have never witnessed anything like it before. I fell up to my waist in a river of mud yesterday, which I thought was just ordinary muddy ground. All of a sudden my feet slipped from underneath me and I wondered where I was going. Was walking from my dugout to the guns, a distance of 200 yards. Found out that this was a track used by the RFA with horses and carts. I was completely covered so had to go to bed in wet clothes.

Somme, 1917

January 1st

Last night I had to help pump 600 lb pressure into the gun, which means about half an hour's hard work. A little while after, there was an escape of 200 lb, so that meant another 15 minutes incessant pumping. Today we have been digging a dugout for one of the officers. Yesterday I exchanged a cardigan for a new shirt. Had another pair of boots, making three pairs in three months.

January 2nd

Went over to the old RFA dugout and collected all the old tins we could find. After half an hour's work three of us were detailed to go to Bazentin and bring a new kit for our Sergeant Major and before leaving we were given a tot of rum each. Just after dinner we were all turned out to shift the shells onto rails as the sleepers had to be returned to the Royal Engineers. At 5 p.m. we went on detachment and stayed until 9 p.m.

January 3rd

Was on ration carrying from 9 a.m. until 2.30 p.m. At 4.30 p.m. we came back as we had finished for the afternoon. On detachment at 3 a.m. we came across a dugout and made some coffee. Had a couple of hours rest and got back to the section at 7 a.m.

January 5th

On rations. Arrived back at 11 a.m. and found the battery being heavily shelled. Left trucks of rations and was told to get right away as quickly as possible. The battery had already been constantly shelled for eleven and a half hours. We were wandering all over the place until 4 p.m. Were told to get our steel helmets and get right out of the danger zone. Stopped at the Divisional for a good time. Had some food and heard the band playing. The cooks also followed suit so we had to fend for ourselves as best we could. This battery has evidently been spotted. I thought we would have it hot one day. We all used to say it was funny that we didn't get shelled, because we always seemed to be firing and receiving practically nothing in return. Were shelled altogether for six and a half hours, putting them all round the guns. No. 4 was out of action as the gun shed was smashed to pieces. An armour-piercing fell just in front of a stack of shells, knocked them over and made a hole 12 ft deep by 20 ft in diameter. Must have sent 300 shells over. Not a man was within 300 yards of the guns and could get a fine view of the bombardment, as we were on top of a hill. Some would not venture within half a mile of the guns after they had finished. As soon as I got back at almost 6 p.m. four others and myself were warned to go on the guns at 10 p.m. that evening. No. 4 gun could not fire; also No. 2 was out of order. All the dugouts around the guns were knocked in so they had to come over here – in our cabush and we put up ten others. Made coffee for them all, which they enjoyed. The Sergeant was coming in to sleep but changed his mind and gave his bed up to another. Fritz was sending over very heavy shells and salvos, four at a time and all in line. A friend and myself were just off the Martinpuich Road and a shell burst within a few yards. We heard that there was one killed and two wounded. At that time the two of us were having a nice cup of tea and bread and cheese in a cookhouse belonging to another unit. We told them a plausible tale and they took compassion on us. Fritz had twelve balloons up observing where his shells were landing. The battery position is in a very bad state with holes etc. and it is surprising to say there was not one man killed or wounded. Our Major has come back to us from England – he will wake things up a bit. The Colonel was round looking at the damage. Now that we have been found out we shall have very little peace. It is comical to see the different antics of chaps running in all directions. Some with no hats and just one sleeve in their coat. The cook, I noticed, did not give himself time to put his on; he carried his coat. While we were away at the canteen I rather enjoyed the music. They were playing all the popular airs. I asked them for 'Bric-a-Brac' but they did not have it. At 10 p.m. we intended firing a salvo but seeing two guns were out of action only two could fire, which we did. One round each just to let Fritz know we are still alive.

January 6th

On rations at 8.30 a.m. Arrived back at 12 noon. In the evening we were called out at 6 p.m. to carry timber from 19th Siege to our battery – about four journeys each, lasting an hour.

January 7th

On rations, back at 11.30 a.m. Another chap and I took the bogey back to Bazentin to unload the rations for the group – got back at 3.30. Have to parade now at 8.30 p.m. to go over with a lot more and dig a cable trench. When finished it has to be two miles long and 6 ft deep. Before starting we had to walk eight miles there and back to get the tools and by the time I get finished tomorrow I will have walked 30 miles. What a terrible night it was – do not want another like it. The heavens poured from 8.30 p.m. until 3.30 a.m. and the wind was so powerful I could hardly walk against it. It was a dreadful night on the plain with no shelter whatsoever from the rain or the shells and only a mile from the first line trenches. About 200 in one batch would dig a trench 3 ft deep and 6 ft long. We would then move still further to another spot and dig another 3 ft and so on. Was simply bespattered with mud and soaked to the skin. When I got back I rang out my pants, trousers and overcoat. Could not wear any of these, including boots for two days – went about without any pants while they dried.

January 8th

As I was dressing I was told to hurry as the battery was being shelled. One chap was still in bed and would not be disturbed. They were sending shells over all day on the ridge in front of the guns. Was on detachment this evening.

January 9th

On water carrying and detachment in the evening. My friend and I were in the dugout on our own until the others came back. A shell struck our section dugout and knocked it in. Luckily there was no one there at the time. They had only gone a few minutes before it got hit.

January 10th

On fatigue carrying planks of wood to a new dugout. Finished at 11 a.m. On the cable digging job again tonight. This was the last time I went down the Heavy Artillery's quarters dugout, which was 35 ft deep and 50 ft long and splendidly made. Arrived home at midnight. Fritz shelled us on the way. The first was a narrow shave, only 20 yards in front of me. I laid on top of the parapet without any helmet as I had previously taken it off to dig. I had no time to take any shelter in the trench and I could hear all the pieces darting heavily into the ground. We were all very fortunate to escape. All the officers bunked off in a large dugout nearby and gradually all the men did the same. We were only four left out of thirty-seven; they had all gone so we did likewise. The officers would find none left. In the excitement some had left their shovels behind, some steel helmets and overcoats. It is curious when one looks at the funny side of it, as even at the worst of times there is always something comical. The capers that some get up to are amusing. There must have been quite 300 men on the job at different places and when I left there could not have been more than 50. It was an ideal night for digging, different to the last occasion. We were filling in a trench after the cable was laid and we must have come across some dead bodies. The smell was abominable.

January 12th

Got up today at 11 a.m. but did not start work until 2 p.m. On guard at 3 p.m. I am the second on, 7 until 9 p.m. Was snowing all night, the road to the lamp was very slushy. The Colonel had a look round today. Finished guard at 3 p.m. This battery is supposed to be going away for a rest in a few days.

January 13th

On rations. Arrived back at 11.30 a.m. Went to Bazentin again to get a load of coal. Arrived back at 3 p.m. Had dinner and were warned about the cable job at 8.30 p.m. It appears that there is a job to find a suitable place for this battery to go to rest because of the very bad weather we have had. On detachment tonight.

January 14th

Paraded at 9 a.m. and was told to pack all my kit and fall in again at 11 a.m. There were three of us left. We started off with all our kit and walked to Contalmaison Circus – four miles away. After a light meal at the canteen we took a lorry to a place called Lavieville about 17 kilometres from the battery we had left, arriving at 5 p.m. There were thirty of us all for the 15th Division Heavy Trench Mortar battery. We all slept in a barn on a stone floor and it was bitter cold. Visited one or two cafes in the neighbourhood and had some fine coffee. In one place they had a piano and it was a proper gambling den.

January 15th

Paraded at 9 a.m. and cleaned the waggons belonging to the RFA to which we were temporarily attached.

January 16th

Washing waggons as yesterday. Saw a French funeral. It was a curious affair as the coffin is carried by hand and all walk to the grave. The coffin is followed by a priest and in front of him a boy carrying a cross. Finished for the day at 3 p.m.

January 17th

Had a good bath today in the next village. It was the first time since my arrival in France, fifteen weeks ago. It is a godsend to have a clean change and a bath. Today I shaved off my moustache. Had a heavy fall of snow in the night. Cleaning out RFA stables.

January 18th

The sergeant in charge of us has gone to Amiens to try and get in touch with our CO. This Heavy Trench Mortar battery is just being formed and as soon as that is done we shall leave. No one seems to know anything about us here. Shifting waggons about all over the place this morning from 8.30 until 12 noon. There is an old soldier with the same surname as mine and our Christian names both start with 'S', so we have to be careful. Washing waggons this afternoon. On guard in the evening at 6 p.m. Finished at 6 a.m. Did our four hours right off and finished instead of two on and two off. Mine was from 10 p.m. until 2 p.m., an awful guard, looking after eight waggons of the RFA, standing in the snow all the time and going on parade again at 8.30 a.m. with only four hours sleep. The worst guard I have ever been on. Did not even have a little drop of tea.

January 19th

Today we were doing stable work and washing waggons.

January 20th

Cleaning up stables and finished at 10.30 a.m. Walked to a village about 2 kilometres away called Henencourt and visited the YMCA there. Saw a splendid *chateau*. Moving today. Shifted at 3 p.m. to a barn next door to where we live. Stayed there for one night only.

January 21st

Moved off at 9 a.m. to Peake Wood and six waggons took us and our kits. The battery formed up in the sub-section. Visited our old battery (37th Siege) today. Heard that we are only here for ten days. We are in huts and fairly comfortable. The battery consists of over sixty men: half RFA and half RGA. The latter is the right half.

January 22nd

Paraded at 9 a.m. Kit inspection parade at 3 p.m. and my sub-section went to a place called Le Sars to make an emplacement for a Heavy Trench Mortar gun. To get to the above place we had to walk seven miles across country and most of the journey had to be done on duckboards. Our living place for two days and nights was an old cellar. There were about twelve men and we had to cook all our food and daren't show our heads above the cellar during the day and not much more at night, as there were snipers all around. We're only half a mile from Fritz. Coming to this place we had to be very cautious as one is easily seen. Each man had to carry a plank, 112 lbs, and I tell you when we arrived here we were exhausted. The officer in charge carried one for a few yards but soon gave it up. He said he wondered how we managed it and he was a great big chap – 6 ft 3 in. Each of his strides were equal to two of ours and we had to almost run to keep up with him. Arrived there at 5.30 p.m. just as it was getting dark, which of course is always planned and it took nearly three hours. Had never experienced such a cold night and coming back the following day the ground was like glass and some were falling every few steps. It was impossible to keep on one's feet for many yards. Of course we wanted to get home as soon as we could and the more we hurried the more we fell. We were tunnelling in the cellar. Never been here before and not knowing how much food etc. to bring with us. We ran short of water for twelve hours. I went on top and collected as much snow as possible and boiled it. It was very deceptive as I thought we would have four times as much water, but it takes four quarts of snow to make one of water. Coming home we passed a Divisional soup kitchen on the Bapaume Road and had over a pint of soup. It was a godsend to us then as it was extremely cold. On arriving back at 9 p.m. we had a bit of supper including a rum issue.

January 24th

Rest day. Got up about 8 a.m. and went to get water. I found I could hardly get any and the only place was the trough, which was 6 inches thick with ice so had to break it with a pickaxe. Even the tea leaves in the dixy were frozen just going 200 yards. Did nothing all day. They have taken all our names for leave.

January 25th

Another rest day. Getting more water from the trough. The ice seems thicker than ever and the pipes are all bound with rag and set on fire. Had a demonstration on the gun we are going to use, a 9.45 in. howitzer. The bombs weigh 152 lbs each and contain 96 lbs of high explosive. They make a hole in soft earth of 30 ft; penetrate 15 ft of chalk and 9 ft of concrete and fire just over 2,000 yards. The report of the explosion is tremendous. Can be worked with four men and an NCO. Had a lecture on the gun and took it to pieces.

January 26th

Had two parcels from home. Went up the line at 4 p.m. and had a hot time going as shells were dropping all around us and there was no cover. One came within 15 yards and the dirt fell on top of us. It was like waiting for death. After a little while Jerry stopped. We avoided the place he was shelling and took a different trail. The officer went ahead and left a sergeant in charge of us. He lost his way and bullets were flying everywhere. I was thinking that some of us would either be killed or injured before we reached our destination. After a good deal of traipsing about we eventually arrived, but to make matters worse we were overloaded with planks, rations, etc. Still, it was a blessing to get there and without a catastrophe. After an hour or two digging in this cellar we had to walk over a mile and a half of slippery ground to a dump and carry a plank each back to the cellar. It was so dark one could at any moment have fallen down a hole. This was at midnight and in addition some of the men had to go at 3 a.m. for a plank each. One old chap, my namesake, got a fright. Fritz was sending over some big shells and while he was upstairs emptying some sandbags with the dirt we collected earlier, a shell landed very near this old farmhouse ruin and a large piece of dirt hit him in the back. He came running excitedly downstairs and said he had been wounded and could feel the blood running down his back. When the officer looked there was just a red mark where the lump of dirt had hit him. I can quite imagine him thinking he was wounded.

Today is the eve of the Kaiser's birthday and a lot of heavy shells were sent over to commemorate the occasion. Further, the 15th Division was being relieved and Fritz knew this. As we were a man short, our officer did some digging etc. He also made my Quaker Oats for me. We arrived home quite safely on Saturday evening after 24 hours of underground work. It is a treat to feel the fresh air.

January 28th

A rest day. Spent a quiet day in our hut. Had another lecture on the gun.

January 29th

A rest day. Saw a Scottish officer buried outside this hut last Thursday. He was killed just outside the dressing station which was near the dump we went to the other night and a dangerous corner. We pass it going to the cellar. I felt very irritable so took off my shirt and replaced same with an undervest. The former was swarming with lice so hung it on the line for a few days to get frozen. Carrying water – two dixys of ice for the cooks.

January 30th

Went up the trenches leaving here at 4 p.m. On our way from the dressing station to the cellar Jerry sent over a whiz-bang, a 4.2 in. It landed right in front of us and we had to get under cover as best we could.

January 31st

Finished work at 12 noon and set off for home at 6 p.m. It took us two hours to walk and we arrived at our hut at 8.

February 1st

A rest day. Had a gun drill and a lecture by our officer, McMullins.

February 2nd

Gun drill and a few fatigues.

February 3rd

Lecture on gun. A few fatigues and collected wood from the old dugout for our fire.

February 4th

Did some washing today. The Australians are taking over our position, which we have nearly finished. Fifteen of them – all drunk. Have gone up to the cellar to relieve a party of our battery who have stayed behind to hand over. Myself and another chap are carrying water for the cooks, getting it from a pump near Beaucourt four miles away. Helped to load the gun into the waggon.

February 5th

Reveille at 7 a.m. Packed up stores and marched off at 9 a.m. for Lavieville. The men with bad feet rode and the remainder tramped it for thirteen kilometres (ten miles). Arrived at about 11.30 a.m. and were billeted in a barn for a night. After dinner, another fellow and I borrowed a bicycle each and rode to a village called Senlis, four or five kilometres distant. Came back, had tea, and walked to Henencourt and had tea in the YMCA.

February 6th

Had another cycle to Senlis today.

February 7th

Walked beyond a village by the name of Bresle – two kilometres away. In the evening walked to a village called Méricourt, via Ribemont, both large villages but the former was the largest. Had tea in the expeditionary canteen in the station – a very large place.

February 8th

On cavalry drill all the morning in a field. It was terribly cold and we were not allowed to wear overcoats. Wood carrying in the afternoon and then walked to Henencourt. Had some coffee in a café there. On parade today the CO called me a bloody liar.

February 9th

Off on rest. Leaving here, Lavieville, at 8.30 a.m. and arrived at Saint Gratien at noon, about 12 miles away. It is a large village where you can buy anything. We passed Lahoussoye and Frechencourt. Visited one or two pleasant cafés and indulged pretty well. The coffee here is really splendid and the best I have tasted for a long while. Just had a nice dinner at 8 p.m. and am now off to bed.

February 10th

Carrying water from a well here, which is approximately 240 ft deep. If I spill a drop of water it takes between seven and eight seconds to reach the bottom. The dimensions of the drum for pulling up is 2 ft in diameter and 6 ft in circumference. I slept badly last night as I was horribly cold; my bones ached and today I felt very queer and weak.

February 11th

Felt cold, shivery and very weak all day. Two parades today. Cavalry drill and a route march – two hours altogether. Went to bed at 2 p.m. but could not sleep half the night because of cramp and rheumatic pains, although I feel a little better than yesterday morning. Had practically nothing to eat for forty-eight hours – have never felt so bad. To make it worse there is no comfort here whatever and the only warmth one gets is going for a long walk. Bed is no consolation as it is much colder than being out. In fact the former is a torture.

February 12th

Parade as yesterday and feeling a little better.

February 13th

Usual parade. Issued with bombs to sew on our coats.

February 14th

Our section on fatigue. Issued with riding breeches.

February 15th

Parades as yesterday. There was some wood stolen from one of the farms. It was reported to our captain so he paraded every man. The wife of the farmer came all along the ranks to see if she could recognise the man who took it but she could not do so. It must have been a man from some other unit.

February 16th

Parades as usual. The officer rebuked me because I was not quick enough on parade. I told him I was not well and had not been so for the eight days I have been here. Went to bed at 1 p.m. yesterday and did not get up until 6 a.m. this morning.

February 17th

Reveille at 6 a.m. Leaving here today. We are going 18 miles and I am riding in a waggon. Arrived at a place called Hemat at 4.15 p.m. Did not leave Saint Gratien until 9.30 a.m. and the journey took nearly seven hours. Sleeping here tonight.

February 18th

Left here at 9.30 a.m. Marched to Conchy, sixteen miles distant and arrived at 4 p.m.

February 19th

Did not leave here until 11.30 a.m. Felt tired before starting. Marched to St Michel, sixteen miles distant and arrived at 4.30 p.m. We got into a good billet with only twelve of us.

February 20th

Had breakfast at 9.30 a.m. and went for a good walk.

February 21st

Paraded at 10 a.m. We were then dismissed for the day.

February 22nd

Paraded at 10 a.m. then dismissed. Went to the town of St Pol, two kilometres distant. Visited a café there and had a jolly good all round feast, the first I have had for a long while. Had some really good tea. We walked home after spending a very pleasant evening.

February 23rd

Paraded at 10 a.m. Had thirty minutes gun drill then finished. Went to St Pol again. Did not get to bed until midnight. The other boys sat up till 2 a.m. gambling – the usual thing when they have been paid.

February 24th

Helping the cook in the morning. Visited St Pol in the evening. We had two fried eggs, a rasher of ham, two slices of bread and butter and a cup of tea – all for two francs.

February 25th

Was on fatigue at the officers' mess, squaring up the guns. Took us about half an hour. Visited St Pol again. Had our usual meal then went to the pictures. Arrived home at 8.30 p.m.

February 26th

Paraded as yesterday. Went to St Pol again and had a jolly few hours.

February 27th

Left St Michel at 9 a.m. and arrived in Arras at 8.30 p.m. The distance was 33 kilometres. We had to wait two or three hours at the previous village, as we were not allowed to enter until dark. This is a fine city. What struck me most was the dearth of poorer houses; in fact I might say with safety that I saw no poor houses at all. They appeared to be residences of the rich and middle class only. All the houses are white and built of chalk. The house in which we are billeted is a gentleman's house and quite large. It seems a shame to see these places knocked about so much.

February 28th

When I woke up and looked around I imagined I was in Blighty. As the windows are missing we have to cover them with rags. There are large mirrors in every room, which is very handy. We are not allowed into the streets until 5.45 p.m., when it gets dark. Went out but not far as it was so dark and there is an everlasting stream of traffic going up the line. The guns etc. that are continually passing through this city is amazing.

February 29th

Shifted our quarter to another house opposite, 36 Rue du Maurice. Went up the trenches from 10 a.m. until 4.30 p.m. only, just to dig a trench. There was a premature on a gun that was firing and a piece hit a house only 10 yards in front of us. Visited the YMCA and soldiers in Arras; there are many of these places.

March 1st

Went up the trenches digging from 9 a.m. until 4 p.m. A piece of shrapnel fell within a foot of where I was standing. It was the closest shave I have had.

March 2nd

Paraded as yesterday and again at 7 p.m. to go up to Blangy (four miles) and where we were making a six-gun position to unload the guns from a lorry. Got home at 9 p.m.

March 3rd

Our section's turn to go up the line for four days. Paraded at 9 a.m. Our billet was strafed very heavily at night. One of Fritz's trench mortar bombs hit the back of our billets and brought down a lot of bricks, making a tremendous report, completely shaking the house and giving me quite a fright.

March 4th

Was digging a position for No. 7 gun. Working from 6 a.m. until 3.30 p.m. digging all the time. Carried up ten bombs after we had finished and placed some in a recess made for the purpose.

March 5th

There is talk about shifting our quarters to a cellar, as it is getting too dangerous. Clearing up the magazine all day. We were making a position behind a *chateau*, called the White Chateau. Last night at about 9 p.m. we were all warned to have our gas helmets ready as there was an attack planned; yet we slept peacefully.

March 6th

Making a short trench from our position to the communications trench. Nos. 1, 2, 3 and 4 guns were firing today.

March 7th

Our four-day shift. Working at the *chateau* until 3.30 p.m. on the emplacement. On the way home a shell burst in the middle of the main street of Arras just a few minutes before we arrived. There were a lot of casualties.

March 9th

On gun pit at the *chateau*, carrying stuff here all day from the RE's yard.

March 10th

Up the trenches working at the *chateau*. Fritz was shelling all day and there were some narrow escapes. A large lump passed right over a fellow's head.

March 11th

At the *chateau* filling sandbags for position all day.

March 12th

At the *chateau*.

March 13th

Lucky enough to get hold of two shirts from a house in Arras. Filling sandbags all day. Had to walk down to the billet in Arras to get the rum for our section and on the way spent an hour in the Catholic club – a fine place. Whilst having some refreshments etc., the piano and violin were being played. It sounded very nice. I have seen some grand players in the army. This place is only about 900 yards from the Boche.

March 14th

At the *chateau*. General McNaughton visited us; he is commanding the 15th Division artillery. Had a look at our work. One of our boys was hit in the arm by a small splinter but it was not serious. Coming home this fellow had a piece of shrapnel hit him on his leggings but it did not penetrate. He was unlucky – yet lucky. He was walking exactly in front of me.

March 15th

At the *chateau* working on No. 8 position.

March 16th

Saw a Jock carried past our cellar on a stretcher with a sack over his head – dead. Another passed with his arm shattered and wounded in the leg. About twelve small men have been transferred to the Medium Trench Mortar. A Scottish officer is in command who was originally in the infantry. Carried up 10 bombs and finished for another day.

March 17th

Fritz is now putting up a bombardment. I am in the cellar of the *chateau* singing to myself so as to deaden the noise. No others are here but it is too dangerous for an attempt to be made to leave while this is going on. Received a photo from Mother. Had a splendid view of one of the enemy's aeroplanes coming down in flames. It was up a good height and was a fine fight. Visited the Catholic club and had some free eatables.

March 18th

The work at the *chateau* is nearly finished.

March 19th

While going up the trenches yesterday our captain was injured. The Scottish officer of the Medium battery took command.

March 20th

Sixty infantry are coming today to be temporarily attached and are taking over some of the positions we have made. Sixty bombs were taken up to the *chateau* today. A gun was taken up to No. 1 emplacement to be ready for a five-hour strafe in the morning.

March 21st

The Medium battery had a premature, killing one corporal and wounding another. Stopping at billet all day today.

March 22nd

Went up the line at 6 a.m. and finished at noon.

March 23rd

Up the line again on fatigue, finished at noon. 'A' sub-section is being relieved at 5 p.m. by 'B' section. One section is on duty now for four days at a time. Having twelve days down the line.

March 24th

The men of 'A' sub who did not get relieved until 5 p.m. did not go up today at all. I went up at 6 a.m. Took 30 rounds to the *chateau* and 20 to No. 1 gun. Saw one of our airmen brought down in flames. What a terrible death. Some say they saw him jump out. Also saw one of Jerry's balloons brought down. There was no one in it. Heard say that it was full of germs, which escape so as to cause disease.

Just come back from the funeral of the corporal of the Medium battery. The old Sergeant Major shed a few tears over his grave – they were both great friends.

March 25th

At the *chateau* until 9 a.m., then carried 30 bombs to No. 1 and 30 to No. 3 gun positions. One of the chaps who was transferred to the Medium was hit in the leg while walking through the trenches. He had to have it amputated and in doing so lost his life.

March 26th

Our section did not go up to the trenches until noon. We were doing a small job at the officers' mess and were finished at 4 p.m.

March 27th

'A' section's turn to go up the line. Finished making shell recess. A fellow of ours was wounded by shrapnel and is going to Blighty. Fell in at 7 p.m. to draw iron rations.

March 28th

Working on a new shell recess. Last night we had a load of ammunition to take up to our guns. The lorry driver did not know where to go so I acted as a guide.

March 29th

Had a terrible catastrophe today. At 8 a.m. we were warned – every available man to proceed up the trenches as soon as possible. After a hasty meal we all went up and in the cellar where we used to stop while on duty, there were fourteen men in this place, a whole section. It appears that at 4 a.m. this morning a terrific explosion occurred. There were about 100 bombs above their heads. The cellar was blown up and the whole house fell on top of them as they were all in bed asleep. We had to start digging them out. Everything was done so cleanly that we hardly knew where this large house used to be; not a brick remained. It was just like an earthquake had occurred. Furthermore, a house right opposite was completely demolished. There was brick dust on the roofs of the houses for 200 yards before we arrived at the spot of the accident. After two hours hard digging we were about to give up hope when we heard a voice crying out. He was extricated from the debris and found to be a bombardier who was getting promotion the following day. After being admitted to hospital he died within twenty-four hours. He must have been buried under all that debris for five hours after the explosion occurred. Another fellow of the HLI was pulled out with both his legs broken and is not expected to live. Some were brought out with their faces smashed almost to a pulp and numerous parts were found: heads, legs and arms. To make it worse, while digging we had to practically walk and stand on the bodies. As the explosion made a huge crater 40 ft deep and 100 ft in circumference, the remaining eleven men had to be left. After hours of searching in vain and then after the elapse of nearly a day it would be impossible for anyone to still be alive. General McNaughton was up and had a look at the damage. It must have been a shocking death for those fellows. It is not officially known how it happened but I believe it was done by the enemy. Probably knowing that we were unloading bombs there every night, he waited until we had a good stock then concentrated his fire. We put up a stone for these fourteen men although they were all over the place. A few months after, I passed the old spot and Fritz could not even let *that* alone. He had landed a shell in the hole and had blown up the stone a few yards away.

March 30th

Deepening a trench and making a new cartridge recess.

March 31st

Yesterday we buried the two men we extricated from the explosion. Strengthened our No. 1 gun position for the bombardment.

April 1st

Came up the trenches at 8 a.m. Working on No. 1 position making the roof splinter-proof. At 8 p.m. we had to load up twenty waggons full of 240 shells outside the station at Arras. As we all came away with the waggons, to be unloaded at our position, one man fell out onto the road. He was taken to the dressing station and all he got was excused from duty for two days. I thought he had broken his leg as he could hardly walk. Arrived home at nearly 1 a.m.

April 2nd

Paraded at 1.30 p.m. for duty up the trenches. Shifted a few shells into a recess and finished at 5 p.m. At 8 p.m. an RE officer came into our cellar. We found a fresh one after the accident not many yards from the other. He placed his listening instrument on the floor with the idea of tracking a knocking sound beneath it. It was reported by a sergeant of ours as he thought the enemy might be tunnelling and we did not want to be blown to eternity. The noise did not continue so he departed and told us to fetch him again if we heard further trouble. This same sound was heard later and is believed to be under-mining.

April 3rd

Paraded at 7.30 a.m. carrying shells again and making a roof for the component parts. Firing twenty rounds at 2 p.m. The last two days Fritz has been shelling around very heavily and sent some very near. I had the nearest escape I have ever had. I was underneath our shell recess when a shell hit the roof and everything fell in. I was not more than two yards away, just a few feet from the end of the recess. There were 200 or more bombs stowed away and if it had been a large shell that had struck the roof we would have all been killed, and that is saying nothing about the bombs going off. We had an officer wounded. Big offensive starts tomorrow. All our four detachments are coming up tonight and there is plenty of work to be done. It is rumoured that there are 19 divisions in Arras (over 400,000 men) ready for the push.

April 4th

Did not finish fatigue until 3 a.m. this morning. Had to unload two guns and put same in position. It was a terrible job hauling the parts about, and we were all exhausted. Today we started firing at 6 a.m., 9 a.m., 2 p.m. and 5 p.m. 100 rounds were fired and it was a heavy bombardment. Could see one of Jerry's villages on fire. It was a grand sight, which we saw from the door of our billet.

April 5th

Are now billeted behind the RE's yard. Fired 100 rounds today, a good few salvos and it was quite exciting. At 4 p.m. our sub-section was called out to fire 21 rounds at a certain target at ten-minute intervals between each. After 14 of them were fired we had to take the gun right out and raise the bed up 6 inches with bricks. With the firing of the last few days the bed was not true. Were relieved by another section. Left at 8 p.m. Fritz was shelling heavily with 5.9 in. A fellow and myself just laid down at the side of the road while Jerry was sending over salvos of 4.2 in. that were exploding on the opposite side of the road. We were hoping against hope that he would not shorten his range about ten yards.

The suspense seemed unbearable. It was like waiting for the last minute to come. We were returning from our officers' mess dugout 300 yards from the enemy trenches.

April 6th

In billet. Got up at 8 a.m. for breakfast. Went back to bed again and got up at noon. At 3 p.m. a large shell, 5.9 in. came over. I ran as hard as I could downstairs and went to see if anyone was hurt. A house was hit just three doors away. The shell made a terrible noise and the damage was devastating. It killed seven civilians, twelve soldiers and four of our chaps were wounded. Two days ago while I was up the line, a part of a shell came through the roof of our billet and wounded a fellow in the next room to where I used to be. Two more were casualties in the billet of ours opposite. There is an 18-pounder behind us that Fritz is trying to discover, which is the reason we are being shelled. The men have all shifted to different cellars as it is getting too dangerous living upstairs. Today, while opening a cartridge box, I found an address of a girl and for fun I wrote to her. She also wished the finder good luck. The name and address is R. Eggleton, 113 Villiers Road, Oxhey, Watford, Herts.

April 7th

This evening we went up the line to relieve the other section and unload two waggons of bombs. A bombardier just went to the waggons and was found dead only a few yards from the billet, 15 mins after he left. Fritz was shelling terribly at the time – salvos of 5.9 in. all around here. It was sheer murder to venture out. He was only 21 and a very nice fellow. He must have been hit with a large part of the shell and death must have been instantaneous. He had a hole in his head as large as my fist and one in his leg twice the size. It looked ghastly to see him lying on a stretcher. Got to bed but had very little sleep as Fritz was shelling us all night. Never before heard such a hellish noise and thought any minute the whole thirty of us would be blown to atoms.

April 8th

Reveille at 5 a.m. Immediately commenced action, then again at 9, 11.30 and 12 noon. Fired over 180 rounds. There was a detachment of seven men picked out to fire one round every ten minutes from 10 p.m. until 4 a.m. Fritz was shelling terribly again and it was suicide to go anywhere near our guns. At last he made a little pause and a rush was made for it. Would not have been a bit surprised if I had heard that they were all killed. Luckily all arrived back OK, yet very drunk. It appears the officer gave each man a pint of rum each. He was in the same condition. The idea was to give them courage – they wanted it badly. In their present state their actions were very comical.

April 9th

I woke up at 4.30 a.m. to hear the most terrific bombardment I have ever yet heard. From our billet we could look along the horizon for miles and see nothing but a mass of flames. Our boys were going over the top at 5.30 a.m. The talk about 'the Great Offensive' had started. We could see villages on fire and mines going up and what not. A never to be forgotten sight, which I would not have missed. Could see heaps of wounded going by. Some awful sights. It must have been worse than hell for the enemy. This is the finish of the battery on this front. In one day we advanced 4½ miles on a 30-mile front. Dismounted the guns in the afternoon at 4 p.m., 11 hours after the advance. We had to walk over the battlefield and saw a good number of dead lying about in all positions; some in a cramping attitude. The majority were Kilties, 15th (Scottish) Division. It was pitiful to see them. Walked to our 1st line: the damage was devastating, with shell holes touching each other. Could hardly tell where the enemy's trenches were as they were levelled to the ground. The officer that came with us found a German Trench Mortar battery that had been left behind. Our Sergeant Major was wounded souvenir hunting. Also, six of our men at the billet were taken away. Left the trenches at 5 p.m. Dug a grave for Brady Gill, who was killed last Saturday, and erected a cross. Outside this spot there were enormous masses of artillery and tens of thousands of cavalry, all ready to keep Jerry on the run.

April 10th

Awoke at 5 a.m. Carried Reely, a signaller, to the dressing station and brought him back again. Supposed to have a sprained ankle. The doctor booted him out of the place. Paraded at 1 a.m. to go to the railway station and help DAC with some shell carrying. They, the RFA, had thousands of shells left over and above what was expended in bombardment, which lasted five days. Got back to billet at 6 p.m. The 15th Division is going on rest shortly. In the bombardment, Fritz smashed up a steel railway bridge to fragments. It was completely destroyed. One of the fellows who was killed in the explosion at the trenches had a letter on the fatal eve to say that his child was dead. He would have been given special leave but the letter was given to the sergeant to give to him and seemingly it was not delivered. It might have been the means of saving his life.

April 11th

Went up the line to get the guns out of their old position and placed on the road ready for loading up.

April 12th

Paraded at 2 p.m. and cleaned guns.

April 13th

Did nothing all day. The RFA had to bury all their dead horses.

April 14th

Have just heard that our Sergeant Major has died in hospital. Was carrying accessories from the RE's yard from Blangy down to the billet at Arras. Met a signaller who was with me at Pembroke Dock. He is on the headquarters staff and yet was always very slow at picking things up.

April 15th

Paraded at 8 a.m. to clean and check stores. There are over 300,000 troops here now.

April 17th

Went to the old battlefield to get some of the enemy's guns that they left behind. Hung about in Arras until 12 noon. It poured with rain all the time. After that we came back to billet.

April 18th

Walked to Feuchy, about six miles from here. This belonged to the enemy a fortnight ago. The ground was very marshy going there. We dug out three German 4.2 in. guns and dragged them across the road, just with our hands, as we had no ropes to aid us.

This is part of the ground taken by us in the first day. Passed the track made by the tanks – quite distinct marks. Heaps of dead horses about: saw five in one yard. A large graveyard here has suffered a lot. The splendid stones were flying about in all directions. Seems such a shame as some are huge and evidently been very well-to-do people buried here. Saw one solitary corpse left in a trench without any head, one leg off and his entrails hanging out. There was only a bone of his other leg left. I don't know if he had any arms or not. One German grave had twenty buried in it. During the advance we took more ground in one day than the three months I was on the Somme. This village of Feuchy was battered to crumbs by our artillery. We are turning Fritz's guns round on his own troops. We have here one of his Medium Trench Mortars captured by us on the 9th. We saw some RFA chaps firing Fritz's 4.2 in. howitzers on them as we came away.

April 19th

Paraded at 9 a.m. and were dismissed to clean up our own rooms.

April 20th

Did not parade at all today. A large number of our aircraft have been flying over Arras the last few days. The RFA in our battery paraded today at 5 a.m. and 8.15 a.m. for fatigues, getting the captured guns out.

April 21st

Was called out of bed at 3.45 a.m. to go on fatigues as every available man was wanted. Walked to Monchy, six or seven miles across the old captured ground. Arrived there at 7.30 a.m. Carried some 18 lb shells from different places and put them all in shell holes away from the observation of his aircraft. These were already for when the advanced positions are taken over. During our leisure time there I saw two fellows laying in shell holes with awful wounds in their heads. Both had all their equipment on and do not know how long they had laid there because we took that ground twelve days previously and I daresay they had been there ever since. While we were all in one of his gun pits where there were four of his guns, I came across two of our officers' suits of clothing. The breeches were smothered with bullet holes and the other clothes were bespattered with blood. Presumably they had been killed by a machine gun, stripped of all their clothing and all would-be souvenirs such as badges, buttons and decorations and finally, their bodies disposed of. In a passage leading to all their guns was a dining room, which contained a large table, two forms, and beds sufficient to accommodate 20 men. After two hours work we left at 10 a.m., being very closely shelled: all the way we were dodging them. Had to shelter in a trench until it abated. Arrived at our destination, footsore, at 12 noon. Altogether, we tramped sixteen miles. Saw some of Fritz's concrete gun emplacements, about 4 ft deep. Was again warned at 4 p.m. for further unknown duties and no man had to leave his billet. Went to the canteen at 6 p.m. and it appears in the meantime all the battery had been taken for different jobs so I was lucky to escape it all. Thought it advisable to keep under cover so went out again through the back entrance and came back when it was dark at about 9 p.m. Had supper all by myself and turned in for the night.

April 22nd

About 8 a.m. one of the boys came in with stragglers – four in all – and it appears they had the misfortune to get lost and so came away home. A few more turned up. It is not 10 p.m. and the main body has not yet arrived. Coming home yesterday I saw an old tank that had had its knockout blow. The party that left at 6 p.m. yesterday evening are evidently stopping up the line. I am away to take rations up to them. Arrived at 4 p.m. This will be their first meal since 4 p.m. the previous afternoon; twenty-four hours up here and nothing to eat. We eight rations-carriers are returning to our billet. The others have to stop until morning. The 15th and 29th Divisions are going over the top tomorrow.

April 23rd

The men returned at all times. One fellow was nearly caught in Fritz's barrage coming home; he said it was simply awful. The Cambrai Road was strewn with dead men and horses. He shelled the road heavily, meaning to destroy and stop our transport. Our friend, while trying to escape the bombardment, was confronted by an Irish priest who tried to console him. He was saying to our friend that he was not a man usually given to fear, yet he felt a little nervous during this 'storm of iron'. These priests are very brave men and do splendid and noble work at the peril of their own lives.

April 24th

Was warned with fourteen other men to parade at once – 9 p.m. I was in the middle of cooking a nice supper and had to leave it. Marched to shell dump, behind the gas works and were packing and unpacking waggons with shells until 11 p.m. Then to our surprise we had to follow three of these waggons to a dump on the Cambrai Road. We were continually unpacking all night. This was the advanced dump and was pretty hot here. Jerry did not leave us alone long. Was afraid the dump would be blown up as shrapnel was bursting just over our heads. It was very cold all night and have had nothing to eat or drink since 4 p.m. the previous afternoon, apart from a small piece of bread. Coming here we were held up all along the road: it was simply choked with traffic of every description going up to the troops. The sky was red with flames and I really felt frightened once or twice in the dark in case we were shelled. Only those who have experienced going up very near the line in an advance and at the same time following a never-ending trail of noisy transport, know what suspense one has to endure. The noise could be heard miles away, never mind within a few hundred yards, as we were. It acts as an encouragement for Jerry to shell this road as hard as ever he can. Further we would go for about 100 yards, then stop for perhaps 15 minutes, and so on.

April 25th

Still on the same job and there is no likelihood of having anything to eat. On account of hunger and cold and not knowing when we would finish, we all decided to do no more work until food was forthcoming. So at 11 a.m. we were finished and marched back to billet, arriving at 12 noon. We had three meals until 4 p.m., including a good rest. Got up at 6 p.m. What a treat to get our stomachs filled and to have a good rest. Was muddled up with the days this week – thought it was Thursday instead of Wednesday. In fact I was so certain that I was right that I made a bet – and lost. Turned in last night at 8.30 p.m. and up at 9 a.m. this morning. I cleaned the room up a little and have got it nice and quiet. The name of the person I saw coming down with his machine on fire was Prince Rupert Charles of Bavaria. Was called at midnight from my bed. Taken round to the dump at the gas works unloading motor lorries.

April 26th

Still at the dump but were lucky as we finished at 5 p.m. We did five hours while the others did eight. There must be tens of thousands of shells at this dump and there are heaps of the latter in Arras alone. Paraded at 11 a.m. after I had had breakfast and was about to have a sleep. Went to the old position and made dumps for medium bombs. Got back at 1.30 and was told to parade again at 6 p.m. Went round to the dump at the gas works and had to take blankets and live round there for four days. Working this job in two eight-hour shifts. The DAC and ourselves are in a nice little house by the side of the Scarpe.

April 27th

Turned in about midnight. Awoke at 7 a.m. and washed in the river. Finished shift at 3 p.m. Have done very little work since we commenced yesterday. Turned out at 5 p.m. to fill sandbags to make barricades between the stacks of munitions.

April 28th

Filling sandbags and unloading munitions. Fritz dropped a shell about ten yards from the side of the house we were living in. It was only a small shell and did not explode. Hence very little damage done, but it shook us up. Wrote to an address: Miss Wilson, Alderley Road, Chelsford, Cheshire. Paraded at 11 p.m. Another chap and I did guard from 1 a.m. until 2 a.m. From 11 p.m. until 12 we loaded up eleven waggons with 60-pounder shells. Turned out at 5 a.m. to load up more shells.

April 29th

Finished at 7 a.m. and slept until 12.30 p.m. Paraded at 1 p.m. and packed some gas shells under the river bridge in case they were hit by aircraft. Did not finish until 11 p.m.

April 30th

Unloading shells etc. Left here for billet at 12 noon for an inspection by General McNaughton. We were rather surprised, as he did not say a word to us. After returning were relieved at 4 p.m.

May 1st

Bombardment this morning with boys going over the top and a general advance on the whole front. Got up about 9 a.m., having a lounging day. Fritz has been shelling about here tonight and a number were killed and wounded.

May 2nd

Went to old position, carried medium bombs and dumped them in the RE's yard. Were doing this until 12.30 p.m. In the afternoon went about and collected all the camouflages we could find from the old gun pits. Carried them onto the roadway by the cemetery to be taken away by waggons.

May 3rd

Reported sick with boils all over my body and a poisoned ankle. It is all swollen and at night I could not sleep with the pain. It is now 9 a.m. and Fritz is still bombarding. He has been doing so since very early this morning. Some of the boys have gone out on the same job as we were on yesterday. Saw the doctor today and only got light duty but everyone thought I would have been sent to hospital. Having hot fomentations on my leg. Jerry shelled here tonight for about two hours. Dropped one next door to the Medium battery. Four or five times we went down to the cellar for cover. I prayed that it would stop and that we should all have a peaceful night's sleep and sure enough, my prayer was immediately answered and we slept very soundly.

May 4th

Reported sick again as the swelling on my leg has not gone down. There is not a sound of a gun to be heard now. Usually it starts about 8.30 p.m. At the above time we saw a huge volume of smoke rising hundreds of feet high and found out it was the large dump 300 yards away on fire. It was not many minutes before the noise commenced with one terrific report and we knew we were in for a nice time as there are a few hundred gas shells amongst them. An interruption for me as I was just in the middle of having a very enjoyable supper. Well, report after report followed each other and the sky was red with flames. After waiting until 11 p.m. we chanced going to bed, although we did not know whether we should have an abrupt awakening. At 7 a.m. when we got up the storm had abated. A very large building 200 to 300 yards long had been blown to the ground with not a particle remaining: you would not know there had ever been a house there. We had the gas alarm at 9.30 p.m. last night thinking these gas shells had gone off but were quite safe under the bridge. Was a good bit of foresight. Fritz was shelling here at the same time as the explosions were occurring. The damage in expended shells is nearly £500,000, as 35,000 shells had exploded. It is nothing to what I thought it would be. Thought it would have blown half of Arras away and killed and injured thousands. Was a very lucky thing it was all light stuff – 18-pounders instead of 6 in., 9.2 in. etc. The result would have been ten times as great. Everything happens for the best and perhaps it will make those in authority more careful and see that the shells etc. are unobserved by aircraft, which was undoubtedly the cause of the accident. Further, instead of having one huge dump, we should have a few smaller well-barricaded ones from 200 to 300 yards apart so that if one goes off, it will save the others. We are now having a thunderstorm, the first rain for fourteen days or more and the first thunderstorm I have seen in the seven months that I have been in this country. Finished a book by Guy Boothby entitled *A Millionaire's Love Story*.

May 7th – 8th

Getting tired of doing nothing. Loaded up some camouflage at Mediums, which took half an hour. Started another job at 10 a.m. at artillery headquarters, winding up wire. Finished at noon.

May 9th

Was at headquarters all day collecting wire. Saw a talk at the station and was going up the line.

May 10th

The result of a court-martial of a fellow in our battery by the name of Bangy was read out on parade. Twenty-eight days No. 1. [No. 1 Field Punishment was two hours a day strapped, spreadeagled, to a gun wheel. Twenty-eight days was the maximum sentence.] He had previously refused twenty-one days. Paraded just after for Kavanagh dump on the Cambrai Road. Arrived there about 12 noon. Commenced work at 2 p.m. and continued until 7.30 p.m. on a dugout, filling sandbags etc. Slept very little all night as the bed was so hard. There is a 6 in. naval gun at the back of us and it makes an awful noise.

May 11th

Started at 8 a.m. filling sandbags and finished at 8 p.m. Many aircraft overhead; 38 were counted in our sector besides over twelve balloons. The sun has been so very oppressive that two fellows here have taken off their shirts to work, with two officers looking on and smiling to themselves. A fierce bombardment was in progress for about an hour this evening, and 15 in. howitzers were in action only a few yards from here; also, a 12 in. naval gun on an armoured railway mounting. I have a nice little bungalow here all to myself.

May 12th

Started duties at 8 a.m. Walked to Arras at 2 p.m. for rations and got a lift back in a waggon, arriving at the dump at 5 p.m. Worked for an hour after tea. Called out at 8 p.m. and unloaded twelve waggons, which took an hour. The remainder of the men had two hours off in the afternoon because of the coming heavy work. Turned in at 10 p.m. and read until midnight. Went to sleep with our clothes on as we were standing by for thirteen waggons to come in some time in the morning.

May 13th

Was called out at 2 a.m. to unload these lorries and load up with empty boxes. Finished at 4 a.m. and again got to bed. Started work at 9 a.m. until 1 p.m. Off until 5 p.m. and worked until 8 p.m., which completed our toil for another day.

May 14th

Sandbag filling until 6 p.m. and then were relieved by another party from the battery. This makes a stretch of five days here this time. Walked back to billet arriving at destination at 8 p.m.

May 15th

Reveille at 7 a.m. Had to parade at 8 a.m. already cleaned up with buttons, etc. After this, mind you, we were sent on fatigue for the

RFA, loading up waggons with manure. After 3 p.m. we could call the day our own. Seeing this town was fortified, I found it very interesting exploring the fort. Paraded at 6 p.m. for a bath, which is considered a luxury.

May 16th

On fatigue helping the RFA again. Went to a concert here tonight. Saw the Bow Bells, which I thought were very good.

May 17th

Doing the same work as yesterday.

May 18th

Reported sick with inflamed, swollen and festered leg. Have just been warned for the Trench Mortar school.

May 19th

Stopped in billet all day.

May 20th

Fell in at 9 a.m. for school. We all jumped into waggons outside the officers' mess. The first we saw of the school was at 12.30, just in time for dinner. Another chap and I visited a place by the name of St Pol, a nice little town six kilometres from here and thirty-five from Arras. We spent a very pleasant evening. Left the above at 9 p.m. and landed home at 11 p.m.

May 21st

We took the 9.45 in. gun to pieces. Learnt all parts, weights, etc. Visited above in the evening. Went to French pictures as the other military cinema is now used as a guard room. A draft of men of 90 arrived here from England to go through a course and then proceed to Egypt to take over a Trench Mortar battery.

May 22nd

Raining all day. Was mounting and dismounting the guns, three in all. It has to be done in three minutes and I can tell you one has to do everything at the double here. They have specially picked bullies to act as sergeants and we are shouted at from start to finish and if one little mistake happens, look out. The man that takes our party is considered to be the worst in the whole school. Everyone is afraid of him and yet, I believe he has a good heart in spite of his loud bark. If we do what he tells us and we do out best, he gives us good encouragement. We parade from 9 a.m. 'til 12 noon, with 30 minutes interval at 10.15 a.m. Then again from 2 'til 4 p.m. with an interval of 15 minutes at 3.15 p.m. The sergeant picked me out to act as No. 1 Captain of a gun and was doing so all day. I'm expected to see that the remaining six men on my gun go through their duties correctly and if they make a mistake, I get blamed.

May 23rd

Took the same position on the gun. The perspiration simply rolled off me today and it takes a considerable lot to do that. The sergeant gave me some punishment and made us all double continually for twenty minutes because one of the men happened to grin at him. When this man gets annoyed his face gets as red as a tomato. Had a lecture on component parts and the 9.45 bomb.

Saw a football match here tonight which was between the school and an armoured train section, very exciting. The former won. They had a splendid team but are very bad losers. It is quite a treat as there are two baths at this school and we can have one whenever we want. Saw the doctor here today and he gave me light duties, so did not go on the gun at all, only watched them. It appears the sergeant made a commotion because I went sick. He sent a corporal after me and enquired after what the doctor had said. I had been taking charge on this gun all the time and he didn't think of letting anyone else have a turn. I got somewhat tired of it, so it was partly my idea to see the doctor, although I *had* slipped and sprained my wrist and had it in a sling.

May 26th

In the morning we fired from the position we call 'the scenic railway'. It is exceptionally hard work pulling this heavy gun up and down the line. Dare not stop halfway up the hill as he makes us go all the way back again, running and pulling all the time. I have never perspired so much.

May 27th

Just hung about in the gun pit. Did practically nothing and finished at midday for the day. Every evening I frequent a little *estaminet* only a few doors away. The proprietress, who speaks good English, is such a nice woman, rather good looking, extremely pleasant and awfully sensible. She has two such well-behaved children. Her disposition reminds me very much of Mother: with a very placid countenance and always the same smile. It is an extremely clean place. It is a wonder where she picked up her husband; he reminds me exactly of a German. He's a peculiar looking man and I did not care for the look of him. I usually have eggs and chips here each evening. Have found an ideal drink for this hot weather: *citron du lait*, for quatre sous, or *grenadine du lait* for the same price. Very cheap and a splendid drink. The majority of the boys here are sleeping in the open, in an orchard belonging to the barn where we are billeted.

May 28th

Paraded as usual and each detachment fired two rounds each and cleaned up a gun that was dismounted. In the afternoon we were all taken to see the holes made by the bomb. Around here the holes are so large that they appear like small lakes all nearly running into each other.

May 29th

Paraded for an hour only this morning. Leaving here, Ligny-St Flochel at 2 p.m. Had to mount a gun on the railway. Had a little practice and fired a couple of rounds. Major commended us and said it was excellent – in fact he emphasised it. This was a sort of passing out test in the presence of twenty officers. Funny ideas the army have. Have now been in the Trench Mortars five months and in the big advance at Arras with practically no instruction to speak of on the gun and yet after all this time we are sent away on a course. Just leaving here at 2 p.m. Arrived at our battery, which has shifted in the meantime to a place six kilometres beyond Frevent and eighteen kilometres from the school. As soon as we landed at 4.30 p.m. we were marched to the officers' mess and paid.

May 30th

The first parade was at 7 a.m. This was followed by physical drill, which continued until 8 a.m. After a good deal of polishing we went on again at 9.30 a.m. and then were dismissed for the day. Had a nice quiet lie in the sun.

May 31st

Usual two parades today. This village is called Conchy, a rather nice one with a river running through it. Another fellow and myself put in for a pass to Frevent, a small town about as large as St Pol. We left the battery at 1 p.m. and arrived here after a walk of two and a half hours. Visited one or two places and altogether had an enjoyable time. This place is very select, what there is of it. It has two picture palaces and very nice shops. Left at 6.30 p.m. and rode back to Conchy in a waggon, which we were lucky enough to get, and it took an hour. At the latter place I slept out in the open in an orchard. It was fine and very healthy and I woke in the morning feeling quite fit.

June 1st

The usual parade. Went to the sports ground at 9 a.m. as we were making jumps, etc. One of the officers was so pleased with it that he gave the men twenty francs. We stopped at a café on the way back: two of us had coffee and the remaining twenty-eight men had beer. There are only three TTs in the battery.

Every available man paraded this afternoon to hear the result of a court-martial read out. There were two men including one corporal and each man had two charges against them: one was for stealing six eggs from a shop in Arras. The NCO was reduced to a gunner and two years hard labour with six months remitted; the other man got eighteen months.

June 2nd

On guard today. While on sentry at about 1 p.m. the General and staff passed and rebuked the men for not standing up. They were having dinner on the grass and did not attempt to rise. I at once presented arms and ordered the guard to turn out. The General was not McNaughton but I had never seen him before and he was heavily decorated.

June 2nd

Finished guard at 9 a.m. Went to Frevent. Found a nice café and had a fair meal: four omelettes, two portions of chips, four slices of bread and butter and a pot of tea. Visited the pictures again and arrived home at 9 p.m. The remainder of the battery went to see the sports, which I believe were splendid. The General competed and won a race. Our battery beat the mediums on their own gun but we lost the tug-o-war. There were several brass bands, 130 pipers and 100 drummers.

June 4th

Gymnastics from 7 until 8 a.m., then gas helmet parade. Went through a chamber to test our helmets. Went here this evening to see a cabaret troupe, 'The Pierrots', which was really grand. There was a female impersonator who was deserving of great praise. He took off a girl so well, that it made him appear very fascinating. The voice, actions and everything were to perfection. Small ankles, cupid lips, dressed very stylishly in an orange skirt, a low-cut blouse and a large black Parisian hat and with perfect teeth and fair hair. It appears that the General had seen them before and asked if they would give us a performance. Quite a number of officers were present, including the Sergeant.

I had a swim in the river yesterday; it was really delightful.

June 5th

Parade as yesterday. Visited the river for a swim.

June 6th

Had to report myself at the officers' mess this morning at 9.30 and was severely rebuked because I wrote a letter home supposedly containing news of military importance. I had quite a different opinion on the subject. I mentioned about the General competing in the sports, and also the severe punishment that was allotted to the two court-martialled men. This letter was torn up in front of me and I was told that they could expect nothing else from a 'Derby' man. As a sort of punishment I was told to be there at 2 p.m. and then had to go all round the grounds of the *chateau* and pick up all the old pieces of paper and tins I could find and put them in the incinerator. I felt like telling the captain what I thought of him but thought discretion the better part of valour and held my peace. Because when I do start saying disagreeable things I sometimes make a clean sweep of it, and in that case it might have been the means of me being sent away for twelve months, which would be rather unpleasant. That is the thing that oft times makes a good soldier turn into a bad one, as the good in us is sometimes equal to the bad in us. Went to the river swimming this morning and afternoon.

June 7th

Usual parades at 10 a.m. Went swimming again in the morning and afternoon. Last night I walked to a village called Flers, three kilometres away.

June 8th

Had some good war news read out to us on parade. Big advance made at 7 p.m. We had a short route march and were told on account of misbehaviour that we are all to have a ten-mile march tomorrow with full pack. Must fill our water bottles and must not drink any water, or smoke. Had to parade at 2.30 today for rifle drill. The men were somewhat mutinous.

June 9th

After the 7 a.m. drill we went on a route march from 9.30 until noon. The officer was pleased with the way we kept up and did not take us so far. Had a bath in the river. Have heard of a great victory: Hill 60 blown to atoms. Over a million pounds of aminol was used, one of which is sufficient to blow up the Mansion House. It is said that the explosion was heard in London, Messines and a village captured.

June 10th

In addition to the two usual parades we had church parade at 10.30 a.m., which was in a field.

June 11th

A heavy storm in the night. It commenced at 11 p.m. last night and did not stop until noon today. Thunder and lightning all night; we were nearly flooded out. My shirt, blankets and everything were soaked. Had to go about all day without the former and had to get the loan of a dry suit and/or coat and depend on the sunshine to dry my clothes. Slept out in the open until about 7 a.m. I feel all of a shiver and cold. The 7 a.m. parade was cancelled but had to attend the second one. Was soon dismissed as it was still raining. Yesterday was my first church service since arriving in this country. Had a swim in the River Canther today.

June 12th

Had one hours' cavalry drill in a field: we got very warm in our steel helmets. Had a lecture at 11.15 a.m. for 15 minutes on general sanitation and personal hygiene.

June 13th

Instead of gymnastics at 7 a.m. about twelve men went for a swim in the river. It is just lovely, very bracing and makes one feel fit all day. This being a running stream, it is very cold and as soon as we have a good dive in, we have a good dive out again. It seems to penetrate right through to my bones. At 9.30 a.m. we all went for a march – six kilometres return.

June 14th

Bathing parade at 7 a.m. for the same party. At 9.30 a.m. we marched to Flers.

June 15th

Reveille at 2 a.m. Bathing parade and inspection at 9.30 a.m. Moving away tomorrow at 4 a.m. Only to carry water bottles and bandoliers. Also, braces down and no coats. The idea of so early a start is to avoid the blazing sun.

June 16th

Arrived at our destination for today at 9 a.m. in Teneur. The march was fairly pleasant and not too warm. Covered about sixteen miles. We are billeted in a large open field like an orchard with a river running through it.

June 17th

Reveille at 2 a.m. Was on guard over two prisoners. After doing about three kilometres, one prisoner fell out because one of his feet was protruding through his boot, so we walked along by ourselves, about six of us. On the way, a sack of boots was found by the roadside and were sold to the French people along the road for a franc per pair. We were lucky enough to get a ride for three kilometres and arrived at our destination of St Hilaire, near Teneur at 9.30 a.m. Walked fifteen kilometres altogether. Our battery were here just an hour before.

June 18th

Reveille at 3 a.m. Marched off at 4.30 a.m. and passed through the town of Aire, a fine place, and landed at Steenbecque at 8.40 a.m. This latter place is in Belgium and is a small but a spotlessly clean village. Was a nice comfortable march of fifteen kilometres. They speak English splendidly here. We bathed here today in the Bassée Canal. It is quite straight, with trees on either side and one can see for miles.

June 19th

Bathed in the canal again this morning. All paraded at 2 p.m. and read Kellay's sentence out for refusing to obey an order. The verdict was twelve months' hard labour. This man is an old soldier, a rotter and a confessed rogue. He was always running a crown-and-anchor board and has admitted to me how thousands of pounds are made by a trick. He had openly remarked that there was nothing in it and if those that were being robbed were ignorant of it, what did it matter. Today it has been showery.

June 20th

Reveille at 3 a.m. Left Steenbecque at 4 a.m. and passed through Hazebrouck and Steenvoorde. In the latter town we halted for an hour and had coffee. Some had two cups each and it was grand. The woman who owned the café treated us all to more than a hundred cups. Another fellow and I had some blancmange. From here we marched to Eecke, over six kilometres. By the way, the above town of Hazebrouck was as far as Fritz got in 1914. After the above we had to go back to Steenvoorde and march along the Poperinge Road for three kilometres before arriving at our destination, which was a field. We walked twenty-six kilometres and all seemed exhausted and irritable. We are only a few yards from the front line. Visited Steenvoorde tonight. Did not stop long as it was late. On our march today there was a storm and we were soaked but soon dried with the sun.

June 21st

Seeing as there was no reveille, I got up at 9.30 a.m. and had our breakfast brought to us in bed. A friend and myself made out passes from 10 a.m. until 4 and got them signed by the captain and then proceeded to Steenvoorde. Had a good meal in the same café we had coffee in yesterday. This friend of mine neither smokes, drinks nor gambles but has a gigantic appetite. After a good tour round we got back at 4 p.m. Left here at 9 p.m. and marched eight kilometres through awfully bad ground to a large village called Watou in Belgium, arriving at 11 p.m. Some slept in barns and some in a field. My friend and I slept in the field.

June 22nd

Slept well in the field until 7 a.m. It commenced to rain so had to rise. Supposed to parade at 9.30 a.m. but had to be cancelled owing to bad weather. In the afternoon we made a bivouac of waterproof sheets and laid straw on wet grass. This village of Watou is just in Belgium. My friend called at a particular café at Steenvoorde where he had been two years before and they knew him well. It is really surprising the splendid English that is spoken by these people.

June 23rd

Paraded at 9 a.m. Put in a pass for Steenvoorde and had a good look round the town.

June 24th

After the 9 a.m. parade, twenty-five of us were warned not to leave camp as we had to stand by for going up the line. Visited Steenvoorde again this evening.

June 25th

Left Watou at 10 a.m. and arrived at Vlamertinge at about 11.30 a.m. On the way we passed through Poperinge. This is a nice camp – all huts.

June 26th

Another fellow and I were called up at 2 a.m. Walked near Sint-Jan, between five and six kilometres from Ypres. Passed the side of it and saw the Cloth Hall; it was still being shelled. Arrived at about 6 a.m. and saw the position. It is all made of concrete and is situated in what is termed 'the tunnel'. The distance there and back is about twenty-five kilometres. Were only 500 yards from the 1st line. The roads here were awfully muddy and the trenches were knee deep in water. On returning I was covered in mud.

June 27th

Rose at 2.30 a.m. and proceeded to the trenches again. Arrived at 'the tunnel' at 6.45 a.m. Fritz was shelling very heavily going up the line. Got back to camp at 10.30 a.m. The men had shifted from these huts to a barn about a mile away. We slept in a hut for one night. Another fellow and I walked into the town of Ypres and passed the Cloth Hall and cathedral. The asylum is a very large building and terribly knocked about. Fritz was shelling very heavily in the town. We thought discretion the better part of valour so we got away as quickly as possible. Tremendously large craters in the above place, supposed to be made by 17 in. shells, 'Jack Johnsons'. We rode back to billet but although risky we chanced it.

June 28th

We got up at 9 a.m. and our first job was to do a little washing. After tea, another fellow and I walked to a *chateau* near Ypres and had a really good dip in the artificial lake in the grounds. This lake was 6 ft deep and there was a diving board. The place is just one kilometre from the above town and it was being shelled while we bathed but we finished our swim. Rode back in a waggon. A party of twenty men went to the trenches to take up bombs. A dump near here went up last night, including Flying Pigs – 9.45s and made a terrific report. It woke me up with a start, although I was very tired as I had walked 30 kilometres the previous day. All the dirt fell on top of our hut. In fact, I thought any second the place would go sky-high. Felt certain that a shell must have burst right outside the door because there was such a lot of stuff hitting the hut. This happened only 300 yards away and it was a marvel that no one here was killed. In this dump there was a small camp with thirty or more huts: they were completely wrecked.

June 29th

Had a very heavy storm last night. A relieving party went up to support trenches to take the place of two others who have been there for three days looking after some 9.45 in. heavy trench mortar guns, which are supposed to take over from the 55th Division. Our Section 'A' are going up the line for two days, leaving at 7.30 a.m. Arrived at 10 p.m. and are working in two shifts. The position we have taken over is a very bad one. No cover whatsoever. Would be simply murder to fire a gun from here. There is a 40 ft deep mine shaft if Jerry starts his capers.

June 30th

Finished work at 4 a.m. after six hours digging and dodging splinters. Slept all day in a recess, which is to be the advanced dressing station for the big push. Started again at 9.30 a.m. My turn started at 12.30 last night.

July 1st

Finished work at 4 a.m. Left here under shellfire and arrived at destination at 7 a.m. The roads and trenches were in an infernal state. Slept until 12 noon. In the afternoon I had a walk to the YMCA about a mile away.

July 2nd

Had a quiet day. Our guns are extremely noisy this evening.

July 3rd

Working on an ammunition dump all day from 8.30 a.m. until 5 p.m. Shifting 10-pounders and generally clearing up.

July 4th

Another lounging day. Six of our boys have gone to St Omer on a course of the 6 in. Trench Mortar guns.

July 5th

Working at dump from 3 p.m. until 8 p.m. Great aerial activity today.

July 6th

Went for a swim at the *chateau*. Left here at 9 p.m. for trenches. We carried up six beds for the 6 in. Stokes Medium Trench Mortar guns, which did not arrive at communication trenches until 1 a.m., after hanging about for hours.

July 7th

Just laid about in shell holes and covered same up so as not to be seen by aircraft. Made for home as quickly as possible. Had some near shaves. Fritz was sending over gun shells and the majority of the men were wearing their gas masks. The smell was similar to strong smelling salts. Rode back in the waggons. Fritz made it rather uncomfortable and the drivers went simply hell for leather and the horses appeared to go mad. Went over shell holes galore and once or twice I thought the waggons were going to tip right over. As a rule, after doing our few days up the line we usually have breakfast in bed and do not hurry in getting up, sometimes not until dinner time. Left here at 1 p.m. for a run to Poperinge. Looked at all the shops, of which there are a good many, and had a really good dinner at a nice restaurant. After spending a few hours here we departed at 7 p.m. for billet, arriving an hour later.

July 8th

A very early day again for us. The boys went over on a bombing raid to see what Jerry was up to and to see if he had evacuated a mile of ground as he is supposed to have done.

July 9th

Leaving for the line at 7 p.m. and arrived two hours later. Three positions were being made. I was amongst four that were working on one and we were only six yards from the 2nd line. By the way, the gun that we are now on is fired from the above trench support and is a much lighter gun. The extreme range is only about 500 yards and the bomb only weighs 60 lbs. All at once a terrific cannonade opened out – a barrage. The infantry here say they have never before seen Jerry put up such a fire. It was only a miracle that could save us four boys. In the middle of the fray I offered up a prayer and it was answered. The straff lasted for fully an hour and we dared not move even just these few yards to the trench where we could have sheltered in a mine shaft, 50 ft deep. This was the worst moment I have ever experienced and considered myself almost blessed to have escaped. Shells of all calibres were bursting so close that a piece of splinter hit me on the wrist but did no damage as it had lost its speed. One fellow with me here had his tobacco pouch penetrated but he had just taken his coat off and it was lying near his head. Dirt from the shells was falling on top of us and I thought any minute I might be buried. The smoke from the above was almost suffocating. After the storm I remarked to one of the fellows that he ought to offer up a prayer in recognition of his life being spared and he said that he had done so while the danger was at its worst. So it appears we both did so at about the same time. It was a great christening and trust I will never again be in such a predicament.

The Argyles were relieving the Cameroons: the former alone had 100 casualties. This started at 12.30 a.m. and finished an hour hence. Our captain took six of us up to the front line to carry in the dead and wounded. They were lying all over the trenches and it was so dark that we were almost falling over them. To get to a sergeant we had to crawl over the dead and on account of the latter and being on the top we carried this man for half a mile to the 2nd line, a mine shaft. He was wounded all over: chest, back and top and bottom of legs. He was brought in about 3 a.m. and was not taken away until the afternoon. He must have suffered martyrdom and every now and again he wanted turning on his side because of his wounds. This shaft is more often than not ankle deep in water and we are continually pumping it out night and day. The sergeant lay half on the muddy steps and half on the floor. After laying there in agony for nine hours or more, the poor chap succumbed to his injuries. This is a treacherous place to get wounded, especially at night. The nearest dressing station is a mile down these trenches and to get a wounded man there at night would take twenty minutes to half an hour, provided the trench is clear. Often after dark there is a procession of troops loaded up with wire, duckboard and a dozen and one things and as two can hardly pass at a time it means that one has to wait until they have all passed. Further, Fritz is continually shelling these trenches, which makes one ten times more anxious to get along quickly and for 100 yards towards the end of these trenches there is no cover whatsoever. In short, all I can say is, heaven help anyone who gets wounded in the trenches at Ypres after dark. It is said that through a prisoner of ours being captured last night while we were having a raid, the enemy gained information regarding the relief party. Fritz also made a raid last night but most of his men were hung up on the wire and killed.

July 10th

Slept very little but as best we could on account of this shaft being so wet and with little or no room to move. In the trenches Jerry could not keep quiet, shelling all day. Managed to get four hours sleep out of two days. At 9 p.m. we had to go to the white *chateau* and bring up two planks each and make two journeys each. We finished at 4 a.m.

July 11th

Arrived back to billet at 6 a.m. after having a ride in a motor from the top of the new wooden road. After breakfast I turned in at 8 a.m. and did not rise until 4 p.m. I went without dinner. Felt very tired and footsore as usual and although very tired after eight hours rest I am going to bed early tonight. One of the fellows who was helping us last night was killed.

July 12th

Did nothing all day but sleep and eat. Heavy shelling last night so the traffic was stopped. We had four waggons of bombs to go to the trenches but because of the shelling they did not go.

July 13th

They have just been round for volunteers for Flying Corps for going up with the machines and dropping bombs on German towns. I said I would go on condition another chap accompanied me. Must not be heavier than 11 stone 5 lbs. They have taken our ages so will have to wait and see. Going up the line tonight bomb carrying for two days. Arrived at trenches at 10 p.m. Started on positions almost at once and finished at 4 a.m.

July 14th

Did not make a start until 12 noon and completed my work at 3 p.m. Did nothing until 8 p.m. In the meantime there was great activity in the air. I counted twenty-six of our planes in one spot and twenty of the enemy's. Our Heavy Artillery and Trench Mortar were very lively in the afternoon. We were cutting Fritz's wire. At 8 p.m. his guns started and kept on for hours with a murderous fire. Was just in time to get under cover. This barrage spoilt us from doing any further work. At this time it was pouring with rain. We had the order at 10 a.m. to make for home. What with the rain and not being able to see our hands in front of us, it seemed sheer madness to attempt to continue. It was a wonder that some did not fall over the broken duckboards and break their legs but all went well, except for falling up to our knees in mud several times. Eventually got to the *chateau* – the dressing station – and stayed there until it was light at 3 a.m. Started to walk home across country. It was terribly slippery and what with the rain and the strong wind in front of us, it was dreadful. I fell over in the slosh five times in a hundred yards as I could not keep on my feet. To make it worse Fritz was shelling and my foot was giving me pain. The fellows were nearly running home and in trying to keep up I kept falling down. Last Saturday Jerry sent over a gas cloud. We had our helmets on for a good amount of time and had a great number of bad cases. It is a new gas and has the smell of onions. It makes one's eyes watery and bloodshot, along with a bad fit of sneezing and nausea. The best of it was that the wind changed and Fritz had to face his own medicine. I came back to billet on my own as I could not keep up with the flyaways. Arrived at 6.30 a.m. and was soaked when I landed at my destination.

July 15th

Got to bed and slept until 4 p.m. A kite balloon was put up very high over this barn of ours with no one in it – just to draw his fire. It was splendid shooting. Fritz knocked it down with the fourth shot by shrapnel. It seemed as if someone was signalling by Helio, until the balloon dropped to earth. It must have been some automatic arrangement inside the basket. It landed right by the door of our barn.

July 16th

The bombardment was supposed to start at midnight last night but was seemingly postponed. A most extraordinary thing. I don't think a shot was fired on either side all night. All the women and children have been cleared away for miles behind the line for this coming offensive. Left here for the line at 7 p.m., arriving trenches at 9 p.m. Was supposed to carry bombs but loaded up two guns on a waggon. They were put out of action the same day. We waited our chance of going up the trenches with eight men's rations. Fritz was sending over very heavy stuff and we were compelled to wait until the storm abated. Gas clouds were coming over very thick, both tear and almond-smelling gas, so another chap stopped in a dugout near the chateau from 10.30 p.m. to 3 a.m. My eyes were running and my nose was like a tap. All the time we were sending over a heavy bombardment. Yesterday it was exceptionally lively in the air; the most exciting moments I have ever had.

July 17th

As soon as it became light we made our way up with rations and managed to get there and back in one piece. Got to billet at 7 a.m. My name had been sent through for this job as aerial gunner. Only one out of each battery is chosen and I was passed by the doctor today for same. Have now to wait until the final papers appear on the scene. There were three casualties in the Medium last night. Sixteen of them had been gassed so reported to see the doctor and three men from our battery also followed suit.

July 18th

Started for line at 9 a.m. but was sent back as there was one too many.

July 19th

Had breakfast in bed and had a walk in the afternoon. Just heard that our last raid was very successful. Sixteen of his battery were put out of action and we took only one prisoner; the remainder were killed. Last night the sky was greatly illuminated by the number of guns firing. I have never before seen the sky lit up so much. It must have been terrible over his side. We had a party who were supposed to go up the line last night bomb carrying, but in view of the raid it was postponed. There were supposed to be fourteen mines going up shortly in Jerry's lines. Artillery Wood is already mined to go up as soon as we start the advance. There were plenty of Fritz's SOS signals going up last night from the trenches. Given the number of his men apparently killed, his infantry could not have been defended very well.

The other morning while returning I saw one of our trench-digging machines. I went up close to have a look at it. At the same time as the 6 ft trench is completed a parapet is also made.

July 21st

Walked to Poperinge and back this morning. This evening I helped to pull in a captive balloon. They are taken almost to the ground by a winch motor. It is surprising how much weight is required to hold one of these balloons down. It took about twenty men and numerous sandbags.

July 22nd

Nothing to report today.

July 23rd

Got up at 3.30 a.m. to proceed up the line – twenty-six of us. Two detachments were selected and one lot fired in the morning.

During the day we carried up four bombs each from the white *chateau*, 1,500 yards from our position. In the latter part of the day we were subjected to a heavy shelling in consequence. While the Medium battery were firing they had a premature: their corporal was killed almost immediately with one large wound in his lungs. One of our signallers was passing this spot at the time and he had four or five wounds due to this accident. Jerry seemed to have our position well in line so we did not fire in the afternoon. In the evening we walked to the white *chateau* and waited there until the 16th DAC came to assist us in bomb carrying. At 9 p.m. only half the number of men came on the scene: the remaining twelve stragglers were found afterwards. Some carried one bomb and some two and we were nearly caught in a barrage but after taking a little shelter we arrived safely at our destination. After this, another fellow and I again visited the *chateau* and stayed there until the morning. Fritz began to shell it terribly. The next dugout to where I was taking shelter, RFA headquarters, had a direct hit. We were nearly buried and very soon came out and found another place nearby. It was the wireless station. Slept very little on account of the awful noise and the cold. Awoke at 7 a.m. and walked up to where the others were and had breakfast. We immediately fired five rounds to register and I took charge of the telephone at the battery end. We hit the target with the second shot. We are to fire twenty-five rounds at 1 p.m. All the men, with the exception of detachment, have to go back to billet because we are having a raid at above time. There is going to be a big raid of two companies of the HLI. We are giving them a gas barrage so as to deceive the enemy. It has just begun and what an infernal row. There are no heavies firing, only 4.5s and 18-pounders. Heard that a Brigadier General of the 8th Division was shot as a spy. We were lucky coming home. Just below the canal, at Salvation Corner, we hailed a passing motor and it took six of us nearly all the way. We put out one of Jerry's new guns yesterday. Heard a new and peculiar sound like the whizzing of a shell. It appeared to be travelling very slowly which I should think was a 17 in. howitzer. It made a noise like the roar of an angry lion. A direct hit would prove very effective. If this shell hit the ground half a mile away it would tremble just like a blancmange.

July 24th

Rest day at the billet. Was tested on the buzzer for this aeroplane job. A sergeant of ours has returned to us from England. He had been in hospital three months from a wound he had at Arras. Six of the Medium were wounded today in the trenches. We put this 17 in. gun of Fritz's out of action.

July 26th

Have heard nothing more regarding going to Flying Corps.

July 27th

Wanted me to sign on in above for four years. The service I have already done would not count and was liable to be transferred to the NAS.

July 29th

Left billet for line at 4 p.m. Fired at 6.30 p.m.

July 30th

Fired 45 rounds and from early morning until late at night we were shelled incessantly. The trenches were in a lamentable state. Fired 130 rounds and had to do runner to and from the gun and OP in the front line besides shell carrying from No. 3 to No. 1 position. Feel absolutely done up. 15 hours of it without a bite to eat or even a drop of tea. Completed out day's toil at 6 p.m.

July 31st

Reveille at 3.30 a.m. and the commencement of the greatest bombardment in history. All guns from Arras to the coast opened out on the second of 3.50 a.m. The noise, well, it was indescribable. No one could hear each other speak unless they shouted very hard. We were out in front of our 18-pounders repairing a road for the latter to advance and it seemed marvellous to think we escaped with only one killed and two severely injured, and even that could have been avoided if the captain in charge had been more careful. One of the latter I saw to the dressing station in Ypres. Those three casualties were due to one shell bursting right in their midst. They had been apart from the remainder of us only about twenty yards distance. During those hours, gigantic shells were coming so closely that it made one count the remaining moments in one's life. We were working right out in the open as if we were immune from all danger. Filling up all the shell holes with sandbags collected from our front line. Later on we were carrying 18-pounder shells for the 16th Division and stacking them up for their gunners. Finished at 1 p.m. and proceeded to our billet at Vlamertinge where we arrived at 3.30 p.m. There is said to have been one million of our men in this attack and tanks galore. Am watching the hundreds of prisoners going past.

August 1st

Before the advance started yesterday we were each given a tot of rum. I must have had nearly a gill. I could not manage it all, it was very strong, and then I was offered more. Was in bed nearly all day today.

August 2nd

Got up at teatime and visited Poperinge where I took the advantage of a good meal. Was charged 1 franc for a sausage. Arrived at billet at 10 p.m.

August 3rd

Left my bed at 3 p.m. and had a walk around after tea. It hasn't stopped raining since the evening of 31st July and the ground is ankle deep in mud and slosh.

August 4th

After rising at 3 p.m. I again gave Poperinge a visit. It rained continuously the whole time but it was a beautiful evening.

August 5th

Ten of us paraded outside out billet at 9 a.m. to work on the dump. We were sent back and returned at 2 p.m. Saw some of the 15th Division artillery coming out of action; we are probably going to another front. There was a heavy mist first thing this morning but now it has all cleared away and is nice and bright. Were kept very busy unloading a train of ammunition, filling it with empties and filling up limbers.

August 6th

Did some washing. Going to have a swim at the *chateau*. The lake was a little deeper than usual.

August 7th

Went to Poperinge in the morning and after tea to get a paper but each time failed. Heavy bombardment last night. Thought the boys were going over. When the 16th Irish Division went over two days ago they lost 700 men out of a battalion. They are now made up and going over, according to rumours, on the 11th.

August 8th

Am going down to Poperinge Road to make waggon lines. Ended up washing them instead. Commenced at 9 a.m. and finished at 4 p.m.

August 9th

Had to move my quarters to near the cookhouse as the water is coming through this part of the barn right onto my bed. A large number of tiles are off the roof due to the vibration from exploding shells. On the same work as yesterday, washing waggons.

August 11th

Working with the DAC all day from 9 a.m. until 4 p.m.

August 12th

Work as yesterday. Had a heavy storm last night. Great activity in the air. Jerry brought one of our balloons down today, all in flames and not far from our billet. I don't think it was occupied. Had a rum issue last night, which is regarded as a special treat by the majority. I usually give mine away and they begin to know this and sometimes half a dozen will clamour round me for my tot.

The great offensive was supposed to have started this morning at 3.45 but was evidently cancelled for some reason or other. For two nights Jerry was overhead at 2.30 a.m. bombing and it woke me up with a start. I heard his machines quite distinctly and they appeared to be flying quite low, just as if they were stationary; no doubt looking for a suitable spot to drop his load. They did not drop very far off and killed 80 men and also a large number of horses.

August 13th

Same as yesterday, washing waggons.

August 14th

Commenced working on the dump at 6 a.m. Unloading a few waggons of gas shells and finished at 2 p.m.

August 15th

Carried out the same work as yesterday.

August 16th

At the battery we were working at, B/70, RFA, there were only six men left for duty. The rest were up the line; also every limber except the twelve that remain here. We had to fall in with this battery and water and feed the few remaining horses. We also did a little grooming. I woke up this morning at 2.45 and heard our Heavies firing away as hard as they could. We heard afterwards that another offensive is in progress. We seem to have him on the run now and glad to say that the weather is in our favour.

August 17th

All our battery is working on the dump today. My turn is from 6 a.m. until 2 p.m. A tremendous amount of ammunition came up in waggons while I was on duty. Unloaded thirty waggons between 7 and 9 a.m. and were too busy to go to breakfast at 8 a.m. Was kept busy, on the go all the time, continually unloading. Two trainloads arrived which made this army corps dump crammed with shells. Had to walk to Ypres in the evening but could not go in the heart of the town as we were stopped and told by the military police that it was out of bounds unless on duty. We arrived back in time to see one of our bombardiers taken away on a stretcher, seriously ill. Washing day for me today. All our observation balloons are shifted well up. One is nearly over Ypres and another over the white *chateau*.

August 18th

Last night Fritz came over on a bombing raid and it was rather exciting while it lasted. Our searchlights had one dead on but in spite of continual firing we could not bring him down. He dropped some not far from here and the rest at Poperinge. Having a rest from work today.

August 19th

Working on dump from 6 a.m. until 2 p.m. packing up shells all day. Saw miles of infantry going up the line headed by their bands; never seen such a lot go up. In the evening a corporal and I had a walk to Dickenbush and then to Ypres and back. Saw a balloon come down here. The occupant jumped out in a parachute with sandbags attached, so as to try it. Landed at billet at 10 p.m. and a little while after Jerry came over bombing and was dropping them within ten yards of where I was sleeping. Thought every minute one was going to drop on the barn. The women civilians commenced screaming which made things worse. Directly the bombs dropped, the people in the barn immediately threw open their windows, which was a mad thing to do as the bright lights illuminated the barn. At first I thought their house was on fire and then I wondered if they were spies. Regarding this, I did not care for them at all and the funny thing was that they continued with their work right up till the last, in spite of Fritz always shelling and bombing just within a few yards of the barn. Fortunately this place was never hit. They used to walk about in their fields milking cows etc. while shelling was in progress, yet never heeded them at all. Jerry's airmen went back as many as four or five times to get fresh supplies. Some came so near that the slates fell off the roof. They must have hung about for two hours and were large in number.

August 20th

Saw a large batch of troops going up the line this morning. Very active in the air. Saw two of Jerry's planes brought down. Am doing nothing today but have to be about in case I am required. I think Fritz has the wind up, to use a popular army term. He evidently expects something great is shortly to occur by his incessant harassing fire.

Left here at 12 noon for Ypres, stopped at the Infantry barracks. Left here at 2 p.m. and walked near our old second line. Helped to dig a long cable trench and got back to the barracks at 8 p.m.

August 21st

Left barracks at 3.30 a.m. for same place. Jerry was shelling the square at Ypres resulting in us being kept back. Had not gone many yards past the end of the square when Fritz dropped a gas shell immediately in front of us, followed by salvos. It was simply suffocating. Had to hold my breath to get on my helmet and thought I would not get it on quickly enough. After waiting for twenty minutes to give Fritz's gunners time to have a spell, we again made an attempt to proceed to our destination but with the same result. The first one dropped only ten yards from us, which was quickly followed by gunfire of more gas shells. Again we had to wait a good time for the gas to disperse, as the air was full of deadly fumes. When we were prepared to advance again we found there were very few men left out of a total of fifty. The remainder were lost for the time being and when we eventually arrived at our post it was found some were coming up in twos and threes. It so happened, after investigations were made, that out of the above number there were 14 casualties gassed and wounded. The work was completed at 8 a.m. and we walked back to the barracks. On the way we saw five horses lying in the road that we had previously tried hard to pass. The horses were terribly mutilated and had seemingly only just been killed as I noticed the warmth coming from their bodies. Heaven knows what had become of the poor drivers. There was one dead man lying in the road. He had evidently fallen as he was walking along with a shovel on his shoulder: he was lying on his face with the shovel through his head.

August 22nd

Working on the dump again from 6 a.m. till 2 p.m. Another man in our battery was wounded today while up the line. An intense bombardment yesterday.

August 23rd

On the dump from 6 a.m. till 2 p.m. Went to the pictures in the evening and enjoyed them very much.

August 24th

Work as yesterday from 6 a.m. till 8 p.m. Then I was warned for going up the line. We are going into action again. Were given two days rations and were supposed to leave here at 12 noon, instead of which it was 6 p.m. before we made a start. Four waggons of bombs went with us. Our destination was about two miles beyond the white *chateau*. Unloaded waggons and each took up a load of wooden planks. After a lot of difficulty in trying to find our destination, supposedly a new position, we found we had got about halfway there. The man who was acting as a guide thought it would be dangerous to take us any further as he was uncertain of the road, so with the sergeant he proceeded to scour the surroundings and left the bulk of the party behind. It was then

10 p.m. and we were laying out in the open with the dead in scores around us that had been left for perhaps a week – as well as barbed wire that we were falling over every few yards. The above-mentioned two men had not been gone two minutes before Fritz opened up. Just before this we had been firing a great deal which made Jerry's SOS signal go up, hence his barrage. We had to leave this spot where we were resting and try and find some cover, which was only a shell hole. The suspense was terrifying. For two hours, we, about twelve men, laid there all heaped together just as close as sardines and dared not turn. Shells were bursting all around us, as close as five yards. The boys said they have never before experienced anything like it and some have been out here a lot longer than me. The shells burst so near that the sparks from them singed our clothes and would have caught fire had we not put them out. One fellow lying next to me was wounded while the storm was at its zenith but I dared not move to bandage him up. He was cuddling up close to me and seemed almost hysterical and was continually crying out. 'I'm wounded, I'm wounded!' and was imploring us to leave this shell hole and find a safer place. I told him we could not do that until the shelling abated which was what happened a few minutes afterwards. I honestly felt that if I had remained much longer under that terrible ordeal of heavy shelling I should have gone out of my mind as it was then as much as I could possibly do to control my senses. Can quite imagine this wounded fellow's feeling under such adverse circumstances. He'd been frantic.

August 25th

We left this hole just past midnight after it quietened down and found a bit of a trench nearby. One fellow, in going to sit down, put his hand through a dead body that was lying there. It being so dark I suppose he did not notice it was just by his side. The smell was awful. We dug ourselves deeper and inwards as a shelter for our heads. It was 5 a.m. before we left this trench, making a total of seven hours at the mercy of the guns. Managed to bandage this wounded man's face, which was not serious.

Another chap in the party was also wounded. The two men who left us at 10 p.m. last night came on the scene with our officer and thought we were all dead. They had eventually found the position and could not venture back to find us, so left it until now. The officer was so delighted at seeing practically all of us safe that he immediately sent us to our billet and ordered that a fresh party take our place. We never thought the same of this officer after that because I think he was shirking his duty to let a gunner lead a party of men to a new position in the dark and to a place he had only been shown once himself. Also, the fact that it was at night while the officer was comfortably sitting in this new position made of concrete. If any of us had been killed there would have been an enquiry into where this officer was at the time and why he wasn't leading his men. There was nothing to help one whatsoever regarding finding the new position. Not a landmark, not even the stump of a tree. Plus it would have been quite easy to walk right into the enemy line. One of the party who relieved us was wounded firing the gun and he was one of the best.

August 26th

Fritz was over last night but did not drop much. Our other gun, a 6 in., is in action and has been shifted back on account of being shelled out. We now have to take a 9.45 up tonight and get it into action. It is said that one or two of Fritz's pillboxes are holding up the infantry so we have to destroy them before another advance is made. We took over two 9.45 guns from the 16th Division.

August 27th

Unloaded our four waggons. We each took over to the Australian position a load of wood, then started to carry over the bed of the 9.45, which weighs over 700 lbs. We got 150 yards, which took seven men an hour. We were absolutely soaked as it was pouring with rain. The rain had penetrated right through to our skins. The ground was treacherous to walk on and we were falling about all over dead men in shell holes. Because of the slowness of our advance due to the weather, bad ground and darkness, we had to give it up for today and proceed to our little den at the white *chateau*. It was by then 10.30 p.m.

August 28th

We rose at 4 a.m. after sleeping in wet clothes all night and proceeded towards the position again. After four hours of terribly hard graft we were fortunate in getting the gun ready for firing. This work was for the Australians and we were going to fire in an open field where there was no cover whatsoever. It took sixteen men to drag the muzzle of the gun. After we had carried up twelve bombs to our own gun and cleaned the mud from it we commenced fire. After a couple of rounds had been fired the officer found that he could not get through on the telephone so I had to follow the wire along to the observation post, and after finding five breaks, I mended it. Twice I had that journey and as I approached the above I had to crawl on my hands for fear of being seen by the enemy and thereby giving away the observation post. Out of the twelve rounds only half were fired as the bed was untrue and we had to stop. Left here at 2 p.m. for the chateau. Had a good meal, the first since 4 p.m. yesterday.

August 29th

Reveille at 6 a.m. Packed up our kit and cleaned the billet. Hung about till 1 p.m. with full kit on. Were relieved by the 42nd and rode to Watten. Finished with this part of the line now. Landed about 4.30 p.m. It is the same farm as before and I am nice and comfy here.

August 30th

Reveille at 6.30 a.m. Dress parade at 9 a.m. and kit inspection in the field at 10 a.m. This is the usual thing when one has just come out of action and all deficiencies are made up. Myself and other signallers were having a little practice on Morse code. Finished at 12 noon. Left here at 1.30 for Steenvoorde. Had some photos taken which were paid for but never had them sent. Another fellow with me also had some done at the same time and he had his all right. Spent a very pleasant evening and arrived back at 9 p.m.

August 31st

There is a football match here today between the Medium battery and the Heavy: the latter won 2–0. Going to the town again today. Coming home I had a little conversation with a boy who was picking hops in a field. He could speak English, French and Flemish. He asked me if I could give him a halfpenny to buy some beer. He was saying he earns from two to three francs a day and he gives his mother equivalent of one and threepence to two shillings. It is surprising how many youngsters can speak our language so well.

September 1st

Dress parade at 9 a.m. Another fellow and myself had a walk around the country and visited a little café where we indulged in a few coffees. This afternoon there is another football match between an RFA battery and a picked Trench Mortar team. It was a draw. Going to visit the village of Watten this evening.

September 2nd

Reveille at 6.30 a.m. Packed up and started off at 10.15 a.m. Marched to a large village by the name of Noordpeene, about 5 kilometres from the town of Cassel; altogether 22 kilometres from Watten. Are in a barn not far from the village and arrived at 4 p.m. after a six hour march with the wind in front of us all the way. It was like a forced march with very little rest. While in bed our officer brought us each a good rum issue. Our waggons broke down and we could not get our kits until 12 p.m. In the evening I had a walk in the village but could buy nothing to eat.

September 3rd

Reveille at 7.30 a.m. Had breakfast at 8 a.m., having had nothing to eat since 7 a.m. yesterday, 25 hours. Dress parade at 9 a.m. and were told we could go into the village after 2 p.m. We were also told to get as much rest as possible as we were going to start at 2 a.m. in the morning, and the same the following day. Got wet yesterday but the strong wind soon dried our clothes.

September 4th

Twenty-five of us left here at 2 a.m. Carried rations for two days and marched to Cassel station, about five kilometres distant. Our party helped to load up one train with horses and after that another. Finished at 11.30 a.m. but started again at 4.30 p.m. to fill another train. This is a fairly large town, very select and up to date. All the houses seem large, very pretty and clean. We are loading up a division of artillery, the 15th. Went on again at 10 p.m. to load up a train, which did not arrive until 1 a.m. After an hour's work we entrained ourselves at 2 a.m. and arrived at Arras at 7.30 a.m.

September 5th

We were in a truck and had no sleep again. We unloaded two trains of waggons, which took until 12.30. This train was extremely long, nearly half a mile. Left the station and marched thirteen kilometres to a village called Habareq. The walk was very tiring, it being such a hot day and with full pack and without sleep. To make it worse we had to carry the rations as well as our kit. It seems fairly comfortable here. We are sleeping in bunks and after a good tuck-in, I went to bed at 8 p.m. Have had no sleep for sixty hours so am going to make up for it.

September 6th

Had a fine swim this morning in a portable bath about three miles from here. I noticed a big improvement in the size of Arras station to what it was before. It has a huge platform now especially for long troop trains. This is a main railhead and you can get to any part of France from here.

September 7th

Dress parade at 9 a.m. Went to see another match between our boys and RAMC.

September 8th

Dress parade at 9 a.m. Going to football again. Our officer is the goalkeeper and it was again a draw. Our battery left here at noon. Passed through Arras and finally arrived at our destination which was a very large village called Fampoux on the River Scarpe about ten kilometres from Arras. When I was here before all this ground was owned by the enemy. In fact his trenches were only a mile out of the above city so this ground is quite new to us. The river was dammed by the French military authorities and made into a canal with numerous locks and we are now at the Fampoux Lock. This waterway is a great help to us for taking up different things on barges and is within 200 yards of our position. On a fine day from our front line we can see the city of Douai, nine kilometres away, which of course is in the hands of the Germans. We are billeted in an old house in this village which still bears the mark of very heavy fighting and I believe we had a hard struggle to make Fritz give same up. We can see the river from our little house. There are just three of us and we are nice and comfortable. We got here at 4 p.m. after three hours ride in waggons. At the present time it is extremely quiet, quite a difference to Ypres. In fact, one would hardly know there was a war on here.

September 9th

Paraded at 9 a.m. for gas helmet inspection. This battery is all over the place in different spots from one end of the village to the other. We are going to have a good look round, which is the usual thing when coming to a new place. One of our officers has just been to us inquiring if we are comfortable and also to see where we all are.

September 10th

Paraded at 12.30 p.m. to go to the new position which is splendid. Was digging a third position and finished work at 5.30. Our gun, only one at present, is in front of Roeux Wood, or what remains of it, and not more than twenty yards from a cemetery. In walking up this trench where the gun is I came across a man's protruding foot. He had seemingly not been buried properly during the advance.

September 11th

We are making a safer place for our gun underneath the cemetery that will take a few months to complete. Am going up today to do some digging from 6 p.m. till midnight. Had a swim in the Scarpe today at the lock at Fampoux. It was 16 ft deep where I was and fine for diving from the landing stage. Helping to bring rations from Cam Valley where the lorries stopped because of being under observation. Took them to our billet, three miles distant.

September 12th

With the signalling class this morning from 7.30 a.m. until noon. Walked to Medium battery where we did a little practice. Only two of us knew the Morse code so we went together and sent each other messages. Paraded today at 6 p.m. to give the boys a hand to unload 50 bombs, 9.45s that are coming up on the river. The barge is taken up to this lock by motor and then to get it as far as we can to our gun, which is quite another two miles, we have to pull the barge along the river by ropes. Sometimes it is so dark walking along this shell-ploughed towpath and this, combined with the sway of the rope, make it very easy to fall in the river. After arriving at the place almost opposite our position, 200 yards across a field, we unloaded bombs and dumped them by the side of the river. Then three of us took three boxes of component parts over to the position. Arrived at billet at 10 p.m.

September 13th

Some of the boys are going on leave. Two have gone today and are brothers. Did a bit of buzzer work until noon. Our sergeant tells me I shall most likely get the hundred francs prize that has been offered by the captain for the best signaller out of the four batteries. Paraded at 4.30 p.m. Walked to where we dumped the bombs last night and carried twenty, 152 lbs each, to the position. The latter part of the journey is up a very short yet steep hill and when I reach the top with the shell it is just about as much as I can do. We have to go over 300 yards and for a man to carry it all the way without a rest one needs to be an exceptionally strong man. As a rule I used to have a halt at the foot of the hill before I made the last effort. There were very few that carried one each, it was generally one between two. You see, each man had a certain number to carry and as soon as he had done that he was finished but with another man helping it took longer. I thought it was much better to take the bull by the horns and get it finished. After carrying half a dozen right off it made my legs tremble like a leaf; it was really hard going. Am told that tomorrow we are going to register our gun on a machine gun emplacement.

September 14th

Signalling practice. Was sending messages on the buzzer to the other boys so as to get them used to it. Finished at 11.30 a.m. Again, we paraded at 2 p.m. for the line and fired 20 rounds on this emplacement and knocked it to pieces. Was great fun at the OP. Fritz could be seen running out and being popped off by our snipers who were in the wood nearby. This OP was in a valley and with the river down below, Fritz held one side and we the other. We were 400–500 yards apart. The officer who was observing said Fritz's men were dressed up as trees.

September 15th

Signalling again today. Finished practice at noon. Nine men joined us today from the RFA reinforcement.

September 16th

Buzzer work this morning. In the afternoon I had a swim in the river. Went to Cam Valley to get rations. Shifted my quarters to a fresh place with another signaller. Two sergeants of the Medium battery have come to us as gunners; they have been reverted.

September 17th

Signalling practice. In the afternoon another fellow and I were making a drainage channel for the water at the pump. Cleaned up the billet and made it look a treat. Have bought a tin of custard powder at the canteen and am having some with biscuits. It is far too thick, almost like a solid block, but it's very acceptable when one is hungry. Two men who were wounded while last at Arras seven months ago have just returned to us from hospital.

September 18th

Going up to the gun this morning. Fired 20 rounds but out of that number we had six dud ones that would not explode.

September 19th

Left here at 3.30 p.m. for Arras. Took the motorboat from Fampoux Lock, which takes nearly three quarters of an hour. Walked to a place just outside Arras to mount a long-range 9.45 Russian gun. It has a range of 2,400 yards compared to 1,100 yards on the old gun. Left here at 6.30 p.m. We rode part of the way back to Fampoux by train, which runs along the towing path from Arras to above the village, arriving at 8.30 p.m. After making some more custard we turned in.

September 20th

Fired 17 rounds today. One of Fritz's planes was hovering above trying to find out where our gun was. Had to have an aeroplane sentry. After getting back I was kept busy barricading the house with sandbags, etc. The officer said it was a very good idea. The wall had fallen down and it was also rather cold in the evenings.

September 21st

Was called at 5.15 a.m. to proceed to Blangy near Arras. It was a lovely run on the boat. We got a load of wood, etc., from the RE's yard and loaded it onto a barge. We made two journeys from the RE to the barge and brought up two or three waggonloads. Arrived back at Fampoux at 11.30 a.m.

September 22nd

Did a little buzzer work this morning. The batteries here have been shelled all day. One of our billets had a shell dropped almost on top of them. The three occupants had a miraculous escape. One was shell-shocked, another wounded and blown out of bed a distance of twenty yards and the third was buried. The latter, after being dug out, was found to have his shoulder dislocated. They have all gone to hospital and they only joined us the other day.

September 23rd

Went to Arras today. Left here at 11.30 a.m. and went to the same place and mounted the Russian gun once more so as to take measurements of the men. Caught a boat back from Arras at 2.30 p.m. Saw a few Americans here today. There is an order out that every man in the 15th Division has to wear the Royal Stewart tartan on his sleeve.

September 24th

Fired 19 rounds today; the target was a sunken road. The General was having a chat to some of our boys.

September 25th

Had a walk to Athies to see about a new billet for the signallers.

September 26th

A little buzzer practice until 11.30 a.m. Am on gas guard tonight. This is a new thing for us as we have never before had to have a gas guard. My turn is from midnight 'till 3 a.m.

September 27th

Fired 14 rounds today at 2 p.m.

September 29th

All the battery shifted from here at Fampoux to another village about a mile and a half away called Feuchy, nearer Arras. Three signallers had to proceed to Arras to bring up the bed of this gun on a barge while another fellow was left behind to look after our belongings and find us a dugout. When we arrived at Arras at 10 a.m., a friend and myself had a good look round the old city. I bought a watch for 37 francs and after a little refreshment we all met at 1 p.m. and walked to where the gun was located. Loaded up same into waggons and unloaded into a barge at the basin. We were told afterwards that the barge could not take the gun up so had to leave it for another time. Got to Feuchy at 6 p.m.

September 30th

Left here at 3.30 p.m. for town. The motor boat took the barge up as far as Blangy but something went wrong with the motor. We waited for a little time while investigations were being made and eventually found ourselves drifting up the river. We afterwards gave up all hopes so got out and walked. After meeting the boat at Fampoux we pulled the barge up to the dump at Ceylon Wharf. Unloaded and arrived back to billet at 9.30 p.m.

October 1st

Fired 14 rounds at 2 p.m.

October 2nd

Had a complete day off and did some washing. A fellow going on leave today said he would call at 22 Fordwych Road (my brother's home) if he had time; otherwise he would write.

October 3rd

Left here at 8 a.m. for the line after firing 17 rounds. Fritz retaliated after we had finished. Some men have been drowned in this river on account of wire being placed at the bottom by the enemy so as to impede the progress of any boats.

October 4th

Fetched rations. Had a little rain last night, the first for over a month.

October 5th

Going to Arras today at 11 a.m. Caught the boat from Athies Lock. Brought up the gun and arrived at Ceylon Wharf at 7 p.m. Unloaded and after feeling our way arrived at the dugout at 9 p.m. It was raining all the time. Had not been in bed many minutes before a sergeant asked me to go up to the position and tell a certain man to come back to billet. I borrowed a bicycle and had awful trouble getting along the road. All the mud accumulated round the wheels and I had to constantly dismount and scrape it off as every few yards the bike would stop dead. Arrived back from the trenches at 12.45, the return journey being quite six miles.

October 6th

Got up at noon. It has been pouring with rain all morning. We are having two guns in action on this sector and two at Monchy, a large village situated on high ground and the two positions are about five miles apart. Left here at 2.30 p.m. for Arras and had to walk all the way. Unloaded 30 bombs from a waggon onto a barge. It was then 5.30 p.m. and as we were not leaving until 6.30 we had a look round the town. Visited the cathedral which has been badly damaged and a huge mass of masonry is stacked up on the road, 50 ft high. After leaving the cathedral club we got into the motorboat at 6.30, getting back to Fampoux at 8 p.m. A party of men had come to relieve us so we walked back to Feuchy.

October 7th

Fired 16 rounds at 11.30 today; it was pouring with rain all the time. Had a letter from [my brother] Charles saying he had been wounded and was in hospital in Newcastle.

October 8th

Was laying out a wire from the new OP nearly up to the front line, to the gun position almost a mile away. Left trenches at 1.30 p.m. to go to billet and carry up more wire. The drum was too heavy to carry all that way so cut off what we considered sufficient and wound it onto a stick. Arrived at position at 3.30 p.m. We continued to carry on where we left off and after two hours we found that there was still a shortage of 800 yards. I was just about soaked as it had been raining since dinner time and I was covered with mud from the wire. Completed our work for another day at 7 p.m. We walked all the way home by the side of the canal. It was pitch dark so we had to be very careful. Landed at destination at 9 p.m. Were working in the rain for over five hours and with no protection whatsoever.

October 9th

Took enough wire up to finish the job which was completed by 2.30 p.m. Again there was a shortage of 400 yards so repeated yesterday's manoeuvres and brought up the necessary amount. Carried wire for a mile this time and after an awful job finished at 7.30 a.m. We wasted over an hour getting the wire straight – D1 – which was very thin and got into an awful tangle. Talk about having to have patience on an errand like this. The things I felt like saying! The more annoyed we got, the worse muddle we got into. Just fancy, a *mile* of wire in a knot, only about an hour to darkness, in the trenches, and having to lay out wire while the light lasted. Altogether there was 1,400 yards of wire laid out in this trench. When I got home I was absolutely soaked. Had to take my shirt off and hang it up to dry. I slept without one.

October 10th

Had to register on this new gun but did not fire at 9 a.m. as supposed. Commenced at 2 p.m. and fired eight rounds which was not a success.

October 11th

Had a day's rest today. A fellow from this battery called at 22 Fordwych Road but no one was at home.

October 12th

Meeting one of our officers at Athies Lock at 2 p.m. After we all met we proceeded to position and fired nine rounds. We have a new OP. I was there this time and it is about 200 yards from the gun.

October 13th

Laid out first wire from OP to gun. All the signallers were on this job.

October 14th

Went up the line. Fired at 11 a.m. and was at the OP.

October 15th

Big bombardment with the Heavies, which lasted until 6 p.m. The noise was almost deafening. Could see liquid fire and Fritz's SOS go up from the trenches. The 61st Division is going over on our lift. It is said they did well and took all their objectives.

October 16th

Fired 20 rounds today. I was at the OP. Out of fear I borrowed a rifle from a machine gunner and shot at one of the enemy. He saw that he could see above the trenches. Our bombardment accounted for 200 dead that were found in one of the enemy's trenches.

October 17th

Did nothing today but clear up for leave. Saw a doctor prior to going home. Waited until 6 p.m. to get our passes. Having to report to RTO at Arras for money. After buying one or two things at Arras we waited an hour or so for the train, which did not come in until 1 a.m.

October 18th

Another fellow and myself had a 'locked in' carriage all to ourselves. Arrived at Boulogne at 7 a.m. Embarked at about 8.30 arriving Folkestone at 11.30. Entrained again at 1.30 p.m. arriving Dover at 3.30 p.m.

October 19th

The Zepps were over London; and had dropped bombs in Piccadilly and Cricklewood.

October 24th

Left for Newcastle on the 10.45 p.m. from King's Cross, arriving at 6.30 a.m. Took a train to Gosforth and called on Charles. Had a nice day today. Left at 10 p.m. for London, arriving at 8 a.m.

October 29th

Leaving for France by the 6.30 a.m. train from Victoria. Stopped a day at the camp at Boulogne.

October 30th

Entrained at above at 11.15 a.m. and arrived Arras at 6 p.m. Walked to Feuchy where we landed at 7.30 p.m. Heard that the previous day we had a premature on the gun: a sergeant and two of our men were blown to pieces and three were injured. It was a terrible sight and there was not a large piece of the gun left. The men are being buried today.

October 31st

Had the day off and did my washing.

November 1st

Fired at 8.30 a.m. and 2 p.m. Nine rounds altogether.

November 2nd

Day free. There is going to be a court of enquiry about the premature we had. Believe this new officer of ours was severely reprimanded. Indirectly I think he was the cause of it.

November 3rd

Fired only five rounds today; one burst in the air and one in the river. Was at the OP and an officer who was new had the wind up because the above two rounds burst quite near us and he was frightened out of his life. I had to go to the corporal in charge and tell him not to fire any more. One round that was about to be fired did not leave the muzzle when the lanyard was pulled and it was found that the corporal had forgotten to put in the charge. Somehow, after that, the fuse of this bomb must have had a knock. It started fizzing and a fellow had the presence of mind to unscrew the fuse thereby saving the lives of seven men. If it had taken longer than 22 seconds, the full time allowed for this fuse to burn, it would have been fatal. While waiting for our officer to arrive at the OP, I had a look down a German dugout in the same trench. It was full of Fritz's dead and one part knocked in by our shells.

November 5th

Fired 13 rounds and out of that number there were 7 duds. The signaller who used to be a sergeant came up with me. We were both at the OP together and he was passing corrections to me.

November 6th

Fired just 2 rounds and both air bursts.

November 11th

A number of infantry were killed and drowned today near the Triple Arch, which goes across the Scarpe, near the position. Fritz was sending over shrapnel.

November 15th

There was a big raid early this morning at about 4 a.m. Going up the line at 8.30 a.m. Did not fire until 3 p.m. when we fired 12 rounds. Mr Pearce said it was the best shooting he had ever seen.

November 16th

Fired 7 rounds today. I could only just hear the orders with the continual repetition. Am very comfortable in our little dugout at Feuchy. Have a nice new bed and a lovely warm stove only a yard away from my bed.

November 17th

Day off. Bought my usual fortnightly supply of milk and Quaker Oats, which does the four of us for about fourteen days. It is usually my job to cook it and one I look forward to.

November 21st

After walking to the trenches I was told there was to be no firing. Five men were killed on the road here while an 8 in. battery was being shelled. The General came up in his car and had a look round.

November 22nd

Was doing telephone work for the Mediums. Was in the OP with Mr Hutchinson, the CO of the battery. Were only about 200 yards from where the bombs were bursting. Fired 47 rounds from 10 a.m. until past 1 p.m. Enjoyed the CO's company very much; he is such a good sort although painted badly by the majority. He has a hard head but a soft heart. Coming up, we were shelled with vengeance with fuses flying about galore and shrapnel overhead, not particular about upturning graves. Have never seen it so hot since I have been on this sector. Had to run from duckboards at river to the first dugout we came to. As soon as we started firing, Jerry soon stopped.

November 23rd

Our wire was so broken that we had to lay out fresh. We then had to mend the Medium's and test it before leaving, which took the two of us from 11 a.m. until 3 pm. While doing this job we saw bodies blown out of their graves. As we left to go home the trenches were being heavily shelled.

November 25th

Too windy to fire today. Again mending wire, which was broken in three places. We stopped at 11 a.m.

November 27th

Again on the same work as yesterday, the wire being broken in several places. Fired 8 rounds at 11.30 a.m. One only went about 30 yards and burnt the camouflage. The communications were so bad I had to go to and fro with corrections from OP to the gun. Both guns are now in the new 30 ft deep mine shaft which has a passage 25 ft long leading from one gun to another. There is also sleeping accommodation for ten men. Mr Robinson reported me today because I had not got the wire between the gun and OP laid out by a certain minute that he had been given for firing.

November 30th

I went to OP, examined the wire and tried to get through. At the same time Fritz put over a heavy barrage and I fairly thought he was coming over and had no weapon of defence. I usually carry a revolver but sometimes chance coming up without one. A lot of shells were dropping along this trench and the wire was cut to pieces and in some places the trench was levelled to the ground. But thank God I got back all right. If the worst had happened we could not have done much as there were less than a dozen men in the trench. Our gun pit was hit so we did not fire.

December 1st

Another fellow and I were coming back from the trenches and had a lift in a private car to Arras where we spent the best part of the day. After a good meal we went to the pictures and in the evening visited the theatre. Arrived back at billet at 8 p.m.

December 5th

Went to the Medium battery to get a drum of wire. Carried it up to our billet.

December 9th

Yesterday I did all my washing. Today fired 13 rounds and later went to the officer at the OP to see what wire there was to lay out. We are having a pig fattened up for Xmas.

December 10th

Went to position and rolled some loose wire onto a drum. Two miles of wire was then carried out for the Medium battery from the officers' dugout through the support trench to their OP and joined onto another line of theirs, which ran from their gun to OP. Therefore, they were in direct communication with the officers' quarters' gun position and OP. This job took until 3 p.m. Fritz was strafing very heavily all day along the road, railway, bank of the Scarpe and the village of Fampoux. There are only five different ways to get back. The above four were out of the question, which left one alternative – the main Arras road, which was about a mile out of our way. Even this thoroughfare he could not leave alone. A shell burst only about 50 ft over our heads. It was a 5.9 HE (high explosive) and the noise was terrifying.

December 17th

Was at the position for a few hours then returned for dinner at the billet. Before returning to the line I cleaned the billet up as it was to be inspected by the General at 2 p.m. The result was that the wire was late in being laid out for firing. That being done, it was found that the telephones were out of order, cells run down etc. It appears that the Medium battery had borrowed our good phones and we had to put up with the inconvenience of theirs. As there was no time to rectify this, we had to run to and fro from the gun to the OP with the corrections while the twelve bombs were fired. It was quite a mess up and one signaller was put under arrest. On coming here this afternoon I was severely rebuked by the Captain for not carrying a rifle with me. The order now is that every man must carry one while in the trenches. After getting to Feuchy I was given one and 50 rounds of ammunition.

December 18th

Was up the line today but did not fire. Last night I was on gas guard.

December 21st

Yesterday was too dull to do any firing and it was exceptionally cold with a hard frost. Laying out more wire. Saw four generals in the trench and one of them asked me how it was that the RGA were in the trenches. He had seen the numerals on my shoulder straps, which made him wonder. Although being in a Trench Mortar battery no one would realise that I was still with the Garrison Artillery. One of the above was a French general.

December 25th

Had a good Xmas dinner. The Captain said that in twelve months' time he hoped we would all be having this meal at our homes.

Last night I was on gas guard. It is now 9 p.m. and snow is falling very thick. Fired 11 rounds. The Guards were about and told me that they were relieving the 15th Division next month.

December 29th

Was seeing that our wire and telephones were all in suitable condition for handing over. Have just heard that a signaller of ours, who was once a sergeant, came back from leave at midnight last night. He went to a shelf in his dugout, picked up his revolver and one cartridge, which was for killing rats. The other occupant who was in bed at the time heard a report and a groan and on going out found this fellow had shot himself through the temple. He succumbed two hours later. Previous to his going on leave he gave me some things to look after, as we were very friendly. He told me to write to his family, which I did but did not get any reply. He apparently lost everything while on leave, all his belongings. Even came back without his overcoat. Before he went away he is said to have drawn out over £200 and I should not be surprised if he had been robbed, perhaps on account of having too much to drink. This was the man who spent a very enjoyable day with me at Arras two or three weeks ago. The other chap who slept in this fellow's dugout would not venture in it again as it had given him such a fright.

Arras, 1918

January 1st

A party of NCOs from the Guards Division were looking round our position, preparing to take over. Had kit inspection and the Guards Trench Mortar relieved us today. Leaving Feuchy and going on rest.

January 3rd

Kits packed and marched away at 10.30 a.m. to a village called Duisans, eight kilometres from Arras and 15 kilometres from here. The ground was very slippery for walking. We are billeted in huts here.

January 5th

Dress parade at 9 a.m. Kit inspection at 11 a.m. In the evening I had a walk to a village called Maroeuil, three miles distant. Had the usual meal.

January 6th

All this battery is going to a trench mortar school. One half to one at St Omer and the other to Ligny St Flochel. I went to the latter where I had been before. Left here at 9.30 a.m., arrived at about 12 noon. There were as many as a hundred men in one large hut, which has 200 beds. Had a good look around the village and visited madam again at the old café, the one that I rather took a fancy to before and she remembered me.

January 7th

Paraded at 9 a.m. There are a few American officers here and they are being put through it; they are even made to double.

January 8th

Three detachments only are picked out among our number and the remainder classified as spare men. Doing the usual gunnery work all day. It is intensely cold today with about two feet of snow. Paraded at 5 p.m. for an hour's gun drill. There were three detachments and I was No. 1 on our gun. Finished an hour later and the sergeant said we did good work.

January 9th

While walking off the square onto the road I slipped and fell on my hand and sprained my wrist. It will be in a sling for a few days and last night I did not sleep as the pain was excruciating.

January 10th

Had a lecture on the ammunition. In the afternoon on fatigue, pumping out water from the railway. Was sending corrections on the range for a battery that were doing firing practice.

January 13th

Visited St Pol arriving there at 1.30 p.m. and went to the café which I patronised last year. After a good evening I left at 6.30 p.m. for the school.

January 14th

It was so wet today that we had a lecture or two in our hut.

January 15th

Pumping water out of railway again. One detachment was giving a demonstration on the gun for the benefit of a French general.

January 17th

The Royal Artillery is playing here in the drill shed. It is quite a treat to hear some music.

January 19th

Left school at 2 p.m. in omnibuses, arriving Duisans at 4.30 p.m.

January 21st

Church parade yesterday. Paraded at 9 a.m. for gymnastics until 9.45; 10.00 – 11.00 a.m. cavalry drill; 11.15 – 12.30 p.m. rifle drill. Football match in the afternoon.

January 23rd

Route march today until 12.30 p.m., then finished for the day.

January 24th

Paraded as yesterday. Had a run to Arras and visited the pictures. Got back at 9.30 p.m.

January 25th

Morning parade as usual. 'Hare and Hounds' race in the afternoon. Had to run eight kilometres and it was 4 p.m. before I got back. Crossed rivers, marshes, and up hills, etc. There were quite fifty who competed but only four went all the way. Some were attired in just football rig. On guard at night, mount at 6 p.m.

January 27th

Going to Blangy to dig gun pits. Last year's Cambrai's reverse has made our people prepared for a repetition. Billeted in Arras. Arrived at 5 p.m. after marching eight kilometres without a hat and a full pack. Went to the pictures in the evening. What a difference in this city to what it was twelve months ago. Now there is a picture show on every street corner.

January 28th

Digging today at the Feuchy Road; having thirty minutes work and fifteen minutes rest. Finished at 4 p.m. Saw *Robinson Crusoe* at Arras. The man who took the leading role used to be our officer. Evidently he was following that profession in civilian life.

February 4th

Went to church yesterday. Was at the rifle range today. Found that all my shots were going wide and could not make it out. The officer himself thought it funny so examined my arms and found there was no rifling in the gun. Apparently it was an old one that had been well worn. Landed at camp at 1 p.m.

February 5th

Walked to a village called Walrus and was back home just in time for tea.

February 7th

Packed up and started for Arras at 9.30 a.m., arriving at 11.15 a.m. Billeted in a fine house in the boulevard opposite the station and extremely comfortable. Went to the pictures. The first night's sleep was splendid.

February 8th

Seven men and a corporal were detailed to proceed up the trenches to 14th Division sector, right of Monchy, about ten kilometres away. Left here at 9 a.m. and arrived at destination at 11 a.m. In a nice deep dugout and comfortable. We are about 900 yards from the front line and only have one gun in action.

February 9th

Three of us left the line for the billet. Walked half the way and the remainder rode in a car we saw passing. All of us left for the new battery that was to be formed, which is composed of all RGA men and no RFA. These are to be made into a Medium Trench Mortar battery. Are at present at a large corner house, not ten minutes walk from the place we have just left. There is one fellow in this battery who was in the same unit with me on the Somme.

February 10th

Dress parade at 9 a.m. after which we went for a short route march through the town. Were all split into sections. I am in the same No. 1 section as I was in the last battery, V15. The 17th Corps General inspected us, General Baron. He is in supreme command of all artillery in the above Corps. I am no longer in the 15th Division; our battery comes under the heading of Corps Troops.

February 11th

Physical drill from 9 a.m., lecture from 10 a.m. until noon and gun drill from 2 until 4 p.m. Went to the pictures in the evening, which are immediately opposite.

February 12th

Parades as yesterday. Took over stores etc. from the 4th Division, whom we are relieving at 2 p.m. Departed for position. Left sector, Roeux cemetery, where we were before. Got the boat from Arras to Fampoux, arriving at destination at 5 p.m.

February 13th

Walked from here to Arras to deliver a telegram to an officer at the billet. This took me half an hour. After getting back I was on gas guard. During my turn I walked up and down the trench so as the time would not hang.

February 14th

Walked to quarry dump canteen to try and procure something to eat. Came back with a good load. Coming back I had a walk through the chemical works, which is a mass of ruins and has seen a great deal of heavy fighting before being captured. On guard again this evening.

February 15th

Was relieved today at noon. Walked back to Arras where I landed at 3.30 p.m. Pictures in the evening.

February 18th

Yesterday I took rations up to the boys. Stopped at night. Left at 8 a.m. today.

February 19th

Today I am on guard at the billet. I did up to 5 p.m. and for two francs I got a fellow to finish my guard until 9 a.m. in the morning which saved me as I went to the pictures and also had a good night's rest.

February 20th

Arrived at position at 4 p.m. On gas guard this evening. Twenty-five bombs came up; five of them were carried from the river to the gun pit. I took a letter to the officer, 2nd Battalion Scots Guards, in a trench near the single arch. It took me an hour to find it. Went way beyond the chemical works. This detachment went down to the billet today but I stayed behind with this fresh party.

February 21st

Laid out a wire to Mark III – Russian gun – OP or rather patched up the old line.

February 25th

Were told to 'stand to' from 5.30 a.m. until 6 as Fritz was expected to come over. No attack was made by the enemy and everything was quiet. This completes my six days up here. Going down to Arras today.

February 28th

Today we drew stores from the Royal Engineers signals unit: three miles of wire and telephones, etc. Was told to see the captain at his quarters at 8.30 p.m. and he said he was giving me a job to take charge of a relay post. This is an exchange situated on a hill between our position at Monchy and the one at Roeux. I am in direct communication between these two places. There are three men with me who take messages to either of the above places. This is a splendid concrete dugout, just like a fort and it used to belong to the enemy. The little portholes, level with the ground, are encased in very large heavy steel doors, 3 in. thick. Am also in touch with the OC at Arras and the Heavy Artillery headquarters. Two reports came through, one for the officer at each position. I have to write them out on official forms and send one man to each place. This is not all honey for these men, because if anything comes along during the night it has to be taken and the men have to find the best way they can to get there. Sometimes they have to wander miles over barbed wire and trenches and sometimes it is so dark that the very idea is enough to make one inclined to hesitate. There is no landmark whatsoever to guide one; not as much as the stump of a tree. In fact, we put a tall stick with an old tin on it to act as a guide for them coming home. There is an old soldier here who acts as cook and the breakfast we had gave him credit: bacon, sausage and meat.

I have to keep practically awake each night in case anything comes through and then to wake these men. It is just like being out in the wilds of Australia as nothing can be seen at all. Last night I lay down at 10 p.m. and another fellow and I were talking about religion, science and several different subjects until we found it was 3 a.m. We had been talking for five hours. This chap was an extensive reader and his conversation was very interesting.

March 4th

Was relieved at 3 p.m. and went across country to Cordide. Left sector; there were no landmarks at all and it was like a large plateau. Walked through heaps of barbed wire and found that we were walking towards the enemy's lines. Luckily we came across three officers who directed us in an opposite direction. After a little walk I saw the Scarpe in the distance and knew I was on the right road. Had to avoid the lagoons and marshes. Jumped across the former where it was narrow and under-estimated the distance and went in up to my knees.

March 5th

Went off with an officer to our position at the quarry. The officer came round at 2 a.m. while on guard and told us to fire five rounds. We were to synchronise with our own artillery as at that time the infantry were making a raid. I had a grand view and it was a fine firework display to see Fritz's lights going up – SOS. We made another raid at 5 a.m. and all had to 'stand to'. I lengthened the officer's wire to over his bed so that he can ring me directly he wants us to fire.

March 11th

Left the position at 2 p.m. yesterday for billet at Arras. Dress parade at 10 a.m. Was up until 2 p.m. getting two buzzers to work. Bought another watch in the town today as the other did not work. Had tea in a café at Arras.

March 12th

Going to position today. Went with officer to see if he could observe for one of the enemy's machine gun emplacements on the right of Pelves but found it impossible so had to cancel the shoot. Two detachments of 16 men are here tonight standing by for Fritz to come over. A double gas guard is posted and 50 rounds is all prepared to send over. He is likely to use gas in large quantities.

March 13th

Fired 17 rounds. On gas guard tonight.

March 18th

Laid out all new wire for both the guns here. I teed into a wire belonging to the wireless people between Feuchy and Athies. It was an awkward job, all underground and very dark. Was relieved after getting back to position at 5.30 p.m. Arrived at Arras at 8 p.m. It rained all the way.

March 21st

An intense bombardment woke me up at 5 a.m. and continued until 11 a.m. On enquiring, I heard that Fritz had taken our front line. On the right, the KOSB have gone over. The noise of our artillery from here was terrific – the report of the heaviest guns was just like an earthquake. It was the biggest bombardment since July 31st last year. Arras has been shelled continually and is still being shelled now. We have a fresh signaller with us making it five in all. He has come from a 12 in. battery on the road between Blangy and Feuchy. An order has come through that no man is to leave the billet until further notice.

March 22nd

Going up the line today. Arrived at 2.30. Fritz has been observed massing his troops here. There is 'wind up' of his coming over soon. Heard that he lost 7,000 men yesterday in his attack. Yesterday, two of our corporals were killed in an *estaminet* in Arras. There were 28 killed with the one shell – a direct hit.

March 23rd

Being shelled extremely heavily on the right sector – Monchy – and numerous numbers of the enemy's aircraft are about. At 2 p.m. we were ordered to get all guns out as quickly as possible. Nearly all the battery were up here helping. We worked relentlessly until 7 p.m. then carried the guns in parts to the river's edge. Loaded them onto the barge and pulled them down to Fampoux Lock. Another part of the gun was in the village and this was also carried into the barge and the whole pulled by hand with a rope as far as Athies Lock. Unloaded everything there and stacked it in a shed, then walked to our billet where we arrived at 1 a.m.

Had a good hot supper which was well earned and turned in for a good rest. We had more than good luck in our favour as all the above was completed without a single casualty. During the time we were working so hard, the officer was continually giving us encouragement and telling us that we would have to hurry as

Fritz was almost on top of us and that we did not want to be taken prisoners. The Medium battery in getting one of their guns in action had ten casualties. From 7 p.m. until we got home, not a single shell did I hear come our way. It seemed that fate was taking compassion on us.

March 25th

Had a good days rest yesterday with nothing at all to do. Dress parade at 9.30 a.m. Went in trucks to Orange Hill where there was an evacuated battery of ours and loaded up 950 rounds – 8 in. into four trucks and proceeded to Arras. Arrived at 1.45 p.m.

March 26th

Loaded up four large trucks with shells. Turned in at 2.30 a.m. and rose at 9 a.m. Had orders to pack up and move off at any moment. After that we loaded up several waggons with stores.

March 27th

Left here at 9 a.m. for a 9.2 position on the railway at Feuchy. Packed up 280 of these shells and took them to Arras. At 2 p.m. we went to another old battery position at Fampoux and loaded up 200 into trucks, which were taken to the same place as the others. Every day we are collecting all the old shells that are lying about where the batteries used to be before Fritz started advancing. Another deafening bombardment ensued all night and I could not sleep for the noise. Have heard that Fritz came over and advanced as far as Feuchy but is being kept in check by the 15th Division, who I believe are 'specially mentioned'. We left here at 11 a.m. Arras is still being shelled and the civilians are leaving. One fellow I saw pass had been wounded by one of the enemy's airmen coming down low and opening out on the troops with his machine gun.

The artillery reserves were tearing up to reinforce. Saw the wheels come off one waggon and he still kept going. Yet eventually he had to stop but it was quite exciting. We had orders to burn all letters, papers, or anything that may be useful to the enemy. Arrived at our destination – Duisans – at 1.30 a.m. Walked all the way with a full pack. Some civilians were coming from Arras, pushing their few belongings along and some elderly women could hardly walk. I felt so sorry for them and it is not the first time they have had to make a quick exit. There is a brigade of artillery that has pulled up here opposite our huts in reserve. Visited the village of Maroeuil and had a good meal.

March 29th

Paraded at 9 a.m. Were on fatigue at corps headquarters at above village. All the battery is to be temporarily split up and men are being sent to different RGA batteries to help during the push and until we go into action again.

March 30th

Had to shift out of this large hut, which had previously been used as a cinema, to smaller ones nearby. Have heard that ten men out of our old battery – V15 – were taken prisoners when Fritz attacked at Monchy. We evacuated just in time.

March 31st

Paraded at 9 a.m. and rode on a waggon to the Triangle on the Feuchy Road and loaded up seven waggons with shells. After unpacking them we came back and loaded up more. On returning we met an empty waggon going up. We got into it and on nearing the place where we worked previously, a shell hit the side of the road, not 6 ft from the wheel of the car. Bits came through the car and I can tell you we did not trouble to climb out – we almost fell out and got in a dugout for shelter. Fortunately, all escaped with the exception of the sergeant who had a few small pieces catch him on the face. The driver also shared the same fate. The car went back to the officer, who by the way took good care not to come because there were a few shells flying about but ran right into a railway after going a few yards. The steering gear and the tank had been smashed so had to alight and left the waggon behind. Had it been a 5.9 or a larger shell instead of only a 13-

pounder, none of us would have been alive to tell the tale. As soon as the sergeant arrived at billet he had to be inoculated – the usual precautions.

April 1st

Paraded at 9 a.m. On fatigue for corps headquarters making a cookhouse. Finished at 4 p.m. four hundred RGA reinforcements came here today for different batteries. Two divisions of Canadians are going over tomorrow to push Fritz back to his original position. Found a leaflet today dropped from a French balloon. It was intended for the enemy as it was written in German.

April 2nd

Work as yesterday. The enemy was shelling very heavily during the night. Just heard that ours was the only battery – Trench Mortars – that got our guns away safely out of the 3rd army. The Medium battery had 14 men knocked out and then did not get their guns out.

April 4th

At corps headquarters again but did not finish until 7 p.m.

April 7th

Saw a signaller at headquarters who was in the same class as myself at Pembroke Dock.

April 9th

Started at 9.30 a.m. loading up lorries with 6 in. howitzer ammunition. There were fourteen lorries and 700 rounds at the RE's yard in Blangy. Finished and home by 4 p.m. Fritz was dropping gas shells in Arras all the morning. Some came quite near where we were working and we had to get our gas helmets ready. Left billet at 8 p.m. with six waggons and went as far as the railway arch at Athies and loaded up 120 9.2 shells. Took them to Dainville, a large dump the other side of Arras and landed at billet at 1.15 a.m. We had an awful job as it was so dark. Had a good rum issue, the first for months.

April 10th

Had breakfast in bed and got up at 10 a.m. At 2 p.m. another signaller, Ennals and myself had to see the captain of the Signallers at corps headquarters. We then proceeded to a place called Wagnonlieu about 8 kilometres from here. We are in a barn with the RE signals near Dainville where we had a walk to this evening.

April 11th

Were all day digging a trench 3 ft deep and about 50 yards long. It was a very warm day. We started at 9 a.m. and packed up at 5 p.m. Moved from this barn to a dugout nearby, which has at least 42 steps and is one of the deepest I have been in. This is imperative as it is used as an exchange where there are numerous cables. Hence no fear of them being damaged by shell fire.

April 14th

Yesterday we were filling in the above trench and marking same with flags so as to denote that a cable had been buried there. Going back to RE near our billet.

April 15th

Paraded at 8 a.m. and are working on overhead cables. Our captain and I had a bit of an argument regarding when I came out to this country. He said I told him a certain date and to make it worse his clerk confirmed his statement in front of me. I point blank contradicted him as I knew I was right. Also, the clerk had put me down in my book as coming out twelve months before I did, which was in my favour. Further, I was put down as being entitled to wear three chevrons and it ought to have been two. Anyway, the officer said that I was a liar and in spite of my continual protestations he said he would punish me for lying. The above I had as a trump card in case he kept his word. However, within the twenty-four hours I again went before him and a sergeant as a witness. The latter at once told the officer that he had mistaken me for the other S. Chapman in the battery who came out in May 1915. The captain looked as if he would like to vanish and said that he was sorry and that he must make amends. Then I showed him my book where the mistake was and I told him I was not entitled to wear three badges. He is a bombastic type of man; jumps to conclusions and never believes he can make a mistake. He swore I was in the wrong and I asked him to apologise.

April 18th

Digging up old telegraph poles at Blangy and loading them into a lorry, which we took back to headquarters. A fellow by the name of Kelly has just returned to the battery. He has been in a military prison at Rouen since last June. He was given twelve months' hard labour for refusing to obey an order.

April 20th – Mother's birthday

Working in Arras near the citadel digging up telegraph poles in the park opposite. This is the central exchange, which had been a large convent. I scrounged a few books and took them back with me to the billet.

April 24th

Filling up a cable trench. Last night there was a terrific bombardment; the noise prevented me from sleeping. It is now morning and a tremendous cannonade is raging, and miles away from the line. What must it be like in the trenches? A dozen or so of our boys have returned from the batteries they have been helping. Some have been to Bethune where they were for two weeks. They said it was a shame to see the civvies leaving the town with all their belongings. Working at Arras. Fritz was shelling it and had to make a quick exit from the barracks. Called at the signals dump at Duisans arriving at billet at 5 p.m.

April 28th

For the last three days we have been digging up telephone poles in Arras. Visited our old battery, V.15, today and saw some of the boys who had just come back from hospital.

April 29th

Our football team played the corps headquarters and we beat them 6–0.

May 1st

Spent all day yesterday winding up wire. Today I went to Wagnonlieu digging a cable trench 7 ft deep. I met with an accident in the trench when a large lump of chalk fell on my head and caused a slight wound. The blood ran all down my shirt, which made me think it was worse than it was. I jumped up and tried to stop the blood with my handkerchief and was beginning to feel faint so got a drink of water. Was advised to go to the dressing station where I had the cut cleaned and bandaged. Finished work at 2.30 p.m. and arrived home an hour later.

May 2nd

On the same job as yesterday at Wagnonlieu. Finished at 4 p.m. and had orders to be ready to go up the line at any time.

May 3rd

Leaving for line at 9 a.m. One position at Artillery Valley, near Feuchy, about 3½ miles back to where we were before. Taking over from the Canadians, who had just finished firing 20 rounds when we arrived. The gun is in the open with no cover at all. There is quite a trench mortar straff today.

May 4th

Were all day scrounging wire and found about half a mile. Left my coat at the position as it was so very warm. Our Heavies are firing a lot today.

May 5th

Was disturbed at 2.30 a.m. by Mr Starling. He said he had been told that Fritz was attacking at dawn. Save the Sergeant – Edgerton – orders were given to blow up the gun if the enemy came over. The officer then went to the other positions to give them the tip. The latter is at Bailleul, facing Oppy Wood. He returned to us at 'stand to' time, 4 a.m., and left at 5.30 when he knew that Fritz would not then attack. Laid a wire from here to the officers' dugout – 600 yards.

May 7th

I 'teed in' from the officers wire to OP on crest by the railway. Had to crawl up on my stomach in case I was observed by the enemy. This place is very conspicuous and high up and can be seen for miles around. Have to 'stand to' every morning with the infantry at 4 a.m. Have two new officers attached to us; one has only just come out in the country. Left line at noon. Walked to St Nicholas near Arras and stopped to have a drink. It was then 2 p.m. and we waited until 3.30 for a lorry to pick us up, getting home at 4 p.m.

May 8th

Walked to a small place by the name of St Eloi, three miles distant. The church can be seen quite plainly which is supposed to be a relic of the Franco–Prussian War. We walked up as far as we could go, 139 steps. A shell had caught the top at some time or other so we could not climb any higher. Should not be surprised if this place has been used as an observation tower as it gives a splendid view of the surrounding district for miles and also stands on high ground. Coming home I noticed a few RFA drivers who were Hindus. It seemed very funny to see them taking the place of our drivers. It appears it is done so as to relieve as many of our men as possible to man the guns.

May 10th

Two of our fellows who were up the line yesterday were

wounded. Going up myself today. Arrived at Cam Valley position at 11 a.m. On gas guard in the evening.

May 12th

I had to trace a light railway running from our gun here to its destination. Started at 3.30 p.m. and arrived at latter at 5 p.m. The distance was about 5 miles. Had to investigate from the signallers there the 'pin mark', which was G11.2000. Walked back to billet where I landed at 8 p.m. Wandered a little off my track on my homeward journey and was completely lost roaming about the trenches. Am sure on one occasion I must have been very near Jerry's lines because from the top of a ridge I was exploring, I could see one or two unknown towns in the distance. I had a chap with me who I left in a trench while I scoured the country but was still unable to find my bearings. I was beginning to get worried as the evening was nearly dark, with perhaps an hour to spare and there we were, stranded on a veldt. Fritz was shelling very near. We had no cover and darkness was almost on top of us. This fellow was more of a hindrance to me than a help. He was always talking about the shells while my mind was on one thing – getting to our dugout, and very quickly. Blow the shelling, I said, when he advised us to stop in a bit of a trench for the night, as by continually walking about one of us might stop one. Besides, look what trouble it would cause to the others and anxiety to the officer. There would be a search party sent out and perhaps some of them might get killed trying to find us. However, to gain the other's assistance I just offered up a prayer, and do you know we were home safe and sound within 15 minutes. It was such a relief. Getting lost under these circumstances is not at all a nice game and not a soul could be seen to help us. There was only one landmark that I could tell I was on the right road. This was a pole placed on the top of battalion headquarters, in a trench right opposite our position. Once I found this mark we mounted the trench and walked across country for about 300–400 yards. Then, again the place where our gun was had no name, that is, I could not ask anyone directions to such and such a place, mentioning some village or town. After all this I said I would go to the officer's quarters and give him this 'pin mark'; he was at a place off the Feuchy Road. After explaining the above I arrived home at 11 p.m. and felt really tired after continually walking for 7½ hours. The Sergeant said he would excuse me gas guard. He was a really good sort, a thorough hard worker, fearless and a man in every sense of the word. Edgerton was his name. I have been in the Trench Mortar (two batteries) with him for nearly 18 months. We have been in some tight corners together and about the one and only place where a man's true character comes to the fore. If they have a noble spirit or a soft heart it is at these rare opportunities in life that they are given a wide scope for developing. If I knew that he was to be up the line with me I used to feel highly honoured and delighted, and oft times it was my thought that if I was killed, nothing could be more noble for me than to do so fighting by his side. He was liked by the majority and no matter what hard graft there was to be done he would have his coat off and work as hard as any man in the battery and never seem to tire. I am not one to give in to anything but sometimes I have marvelled at his pluck and bulldog grit.

A better sportsman could not be found. He was a good footballer and in fact he could compete in anything. He was quite a young fellow of 23 and had been a miner in civilian life.

May 13th

Everyone, with the exception of two men had to leave at 8 a.m. and proceed to the other position at Artillery Valley, Athies. Had to carry a sub-bed of the Mark III gun from the roadway where it was dumped, to a position 60 yards away. Put this on an old barrow, which we pulled along with ropes. It was an awful job as there were shell holes up hill and down dale – in fact a very hard job. Took up four loads and it is now 2.30 p.m. After all this trouble they are undecided over whether the gun is to be mounted here or on the other side of the railway arch 600 yards further down. In the meantime, the gun at Cam Valley position is being dismantled and taken down on the light railway and thence to a new place in Tilloy Wood on the Cambrai–Arras Road. That is why I had to trace this railway line to see where it ended so as to get the gun to its fresh position. It is now 9 p.m. and they have just decided to place the gun this side of the arch. We worked for an hour then finished our day's toil. It has been raining nearly all the time, which tends to make the work much harder.

May 14th

This gun has to be prepared for firing by 4 p.m. Woke up this morning feeling more dead than alive. Think I must have a touch of flu. There is a long job today from 4 a.m. until 3 p.m. in helping them to get the gun ready. Last night while carrying up parts of the gun it was raining and Sergeant Edgerton was not looking very well so I took pity on him and lent him my leather waistcoat. Hence me getting soaked after hours working in the open. I had to lay out 1,500 yards of wire after this. Had some given me which only carried half the distance required, so had to scrounge the remainder. I managed to crawl back at 7.30 p.m. absolutely whacked, dead beat to the world; the worst I have felt since the Somme eighteen months ago. Had a good rum issue and turned in about ten minutes after. Was supposed to report to Mr Starling on how far I had got with the wiring but for the life of me I could not walk another four miles, so my friend Ennals took my place, for which I was very grateful. I arose at 8 a.m. feeling very heavy about the head but in the body a little rested.

May 15th

Yesterday, Fritz had a direct hit on the gun pit here. Ennals had a miraculous escape as at the time he was adjusting the gun yet did not have a scratch. Ennals and I are supposed to scrounge the remaining 1,000 yards of wire to finish the above job. We got relieved at 11.30. The heat is very oppressive and have four miles to walk to February Circus where we get the lorry to take us the remaining seven or eight miles. After getting home at 1.30, I could not eat any dinner, only managing a cup of tea before going straight to bed. My friend was going to the village and I asked him to get me a bottle of champagne: all I wanted was drink and I just fancied champagne and slept with it at my head.

May 17th

Felt much better today thanks to the champagne – drank it all. Had a walk to Duisans to get the photos I had taken over a week ago including the one with Mother in the corner. The young ladies there took quite a fancy to it and said, 'Is that your wife?' After this I took a nice book and had a pleasant few hours reading in a picturesque spot nearby.

May 18th

Feel my real self again today. Going up the line at 9 a.m. and taking one mile of wire with us and I know what that means. Went to Tilloy Wood and laid out a wire from their dugout to a 'bury' in a test box off Cambrai Road. Arrived at my dugout at 4 p.m. to meet the lorry. I am staying in a dugout just by the officers. Am working an exchange with the assistance of another man. I am in touch with the positions at Tilloy Wood, Artillery Valley and Bailleul. Also the headquarters 9 kilometres away, where the captain is. Now and again I have a run round to these places to give the boys a look up and test their wires and tele-phones. Going back to billet at Duisans.

May 20th

Shifted our exchange to Sunken Road, near Athies. Took up a new switchboard, which was rigged up. After this I went to the gun at Tilloy. Commenced laying out a wire to a new OP in the above village but after a little while found there was not enough to complete the work. So instead of a double line I had a single one and an earth return. That is, the return current will have to travel through earth instead of through the wire. This is a thing usually resorted to when there is a shortage of wire, but it is not the safest as it is quite possible for the enemy to pick up all this information with special instruments designed for that purpose. We have to be very careful as Fritz picks up a great deal of news like this, daily. We fired two rounds and had tea with the boys. The officer and I returned at 9 p.m. Have to sleep with the receiver of the telephone at my ear. In fact I have slept with the watch receiver round my head but this is rather awkward. A new officer came up today; they have two days up only.

May 22nd

Ennals and I unteed a wire that ran to the 47th battery, code 'HUNO' and made a complete line with a separate terminal on their switchboard. We used to have trouble in getting through to this battery because it was an indirect line. If we could not get these people we could hardly get anyone, as they used to get us through to many places. Relieved and got home at 11 a.m. Had a letter from Mother telling me about a raid, the nearest they have had. A dud demolished the Carlton Hotel opposite to where she lives.

May 27th

Up again today. My few days down were as usual very comfortable and I took all the rest that was possible. I could have had my pick of a companion to take up with me. My choice of any was a fellow named Pembleton; a very interesting man to talk to and well read. A willing worker but very slow. Mr Ratray started to walk to Tilloy but found Fritz was shelling in the direction of Devils and Tilloy Woods, also Cambrai Road. The journey was all across country with no cover. Went back and decided to go after tea, arriving at about 6 p.m., but did not have it all our own way. All positions were given instructions of what to do if Jerry should come over.

May 28th

Expected Fritz over again this morning but nothing occurred. I had my 'running shoes' ready, to quote Mr Starling's words. He is very nice and extremely witty. He has such dry sayings and makes me roar at times and is a really amusing character. They were having it hot at Tilloy last night. About 11 p.m. I went out and had a look. Fritz's SOS signals were going up and they say we are making a raid, which accounts for it. Fired 4 rounds at above position. The enemy had a balloon up, facing us. To get into communication with our captain from my exchange I have to go through four others and this takes the best part of an hour.

May 30th

Could not get through on any of the lines today so took my companion to examine all the lines and from 10 a.m. until 9 p.m. I was continually looking for breaks in the wires. Eventually had to lay out a new line to this 47th battery and in half an hour's time I was in touch with all. Shells were dropping round us here all day. Twelve of the Jocks were wounded. One of the boys was bringing up our rations along this Sunken Road. He heard a shell coming and fell down a dugout nearby – he did not stop to walk down. The shell exploded and blew up the rations he was trailing after him but he escaped with just a fright. The fellow came up to us with what remained of the food together with the pickles running into the tea and the jam into the cheese. Still, we managed to arrange it all right. The poor fellow looked very white and scared. Being relieved in the morning.

June 4th

Nothing much to report for the last few days of my rest at the billet. When I arrived at the trenches today, Fritz was sending over 'HE', right over our dugout. He completely shelled out a 4.5 in. battery; a battery with whom I am in communication. All day Fritz was concentrating on them with 5.9 in. One of our fellows, a new relief, was killed while changing over at Tilloy. There seemingly was a fight in the air and a stray bullet killed him instantly. He was an old soldier with about 24 years service and had been out here since the beginning. It was the same aeroplane that was spotted above 4.5 in. battery. Went with an officer to battalion headquarters to see about running out a fresh line from our gun to an OP in the trench. After this I walked to Artillery Valley and carried away half a reel of wire to my dugout.

June 5th

Left here at 9.30 a.m. with two reels of wire and all necessary requisites. Walked to battalion headquarters where I was met by an infantry signaller. Left him here while I ran a line from our gun, intending to meet him with it but found there was a shortage of 400 yards. Went to infantry divisional OP then came back to

Cambrai Road and took the line up to a company in the supports. Fixed it up and finally okayed the line. Walked back to my dugout. I have had this journey twice today and at 8 p.m. I have to go to an infantry dugout near supports and sleep there all night. I laid on the floor but did not sleep. It was too cold and I did not have any blankets so it was a case of trying to sleep in a sitting position.

June 6th

Was up at 3.30 a.m. I teed my wire into their OP line and called up RA at 3.40 a.m. but all in vain. Eventually got through at 4.10. The line from RA to our battery was damaged so had to wait while it was mended. At 4.45 firing commenced. Expended 12 rounds by 6.30 a.m. after being nearly out of this OP. While we were firing, Jerry's balloon and aeroplanes were up. He shelled for a good time afterwards all round the trenches. It was 7.30 before we could think of leaving. After having breakfast with the boys at the gun I left at 9 a.m. arriving at my home an hour later. Had a good clean up which I badly needed after being out all night.

June 8th

Was mending wires again yesterday. In the afternoon went to Artillery Valley and fired 6 rounds. Relieved today at 11 a.m. Got home at dinner time. I had a look round the village in the evening.

June 10th

Digging a cable trench at the *chateau*, general headquarters in 'Maroeuil'. Went shopping in the village after work and bought some eatables.

June 14th

Went to battalion headquarters. Saw a signaller corporal of the Middlesex and asked him if an improvement could be made to reduce the quantity of open wire from our gun to their decoy. Went with a signaller to the front line, Tilloy Trench 3rd company, and found a bury which ran from there to battalion headquarters. I fixed a line from our gun to the latter, joined the two together and thereby have a direct wire from position to front line.

June 15th

Saw the infantry corporal again today. We have to disconnect one of the above and are given another in its place. The 15th Division have come out from the left sector and have been replaced by the 51st Division, the former having a month's rest. Relieved today and visited the village of Maroeuil.

June 20th

Our supposed rest days were occupied by making splinter-proof huts.

June 24th

At positions again. Another signaller is stopping up for a day to help me with some cable. After dinner we walked to Tilloy to try and get through on the buried line but found Fritz had registered this route so of course gave up the job and went back to our dugout. Going to fire 30 rounds from the Tilloy position. We had to give up the OP near the front line that we intended using because of Fritz shelling, so observed from one lower down the trench. Finished our shoot at 8 p.m. after 2½ hours. That little affair cost £229 10s 0d. A Brigadier General was killed in a trench facing our gun at Artillery Valley. Three of our men were asked to give a hand and when they went round found this officer blown to pieces and had to be left there for that reason. He was a highly decorated man including the Victoria Cross and his name was Alfred Forbes Lumsden, DSO.

Returned to billet.

June 25th

Cycled up the line to take a message to Mr Ratray.

June 28th

The previous few days have been occupied by taking rations to the boys in the trenches. Going up myself today. The heavy shelling woke me up at 2 a.m. this morning. Went out and repaired the line. Fired 40 rounds from Tilloy gun. I was at battalion headquarters transmitting the corrections to the gun but found we could not make anyone hear. I guessed something had happened so while the two officers and myself were going back we were confronted by two men who told us they had had a premature. There was one who had internal concussion, the corporal with a broken arm and another who was not found until the following day in a trench 20 yards away with his head and arm missing.

July 1st

Relieved a day earlier this time because of the above accident. Our captain, on being told of this premature by one of our men, rebuked him because he had no puttees on. He told him he would have to smarten his ideas up, as if to say that an accident like this was nothing compared to going about 'improperly dressed'. This fellow was covered with blood and had had a thorough fright. I was stunned when the officer passed this remark. The same fellow has not forgotten it. He felt as if he could have knocked him down. The man who had concussion is dying. Had a letter from the brother of the man who shot himself, asking for particulars. The chap who was killed by the premature was buried at Arras cemetery today. Coming back we came across an old French civilian and we made a collection for the old boy. He must have been over eighty and was so weak he could hardly pick the money up.

July 3rd

Returning from a fatigue today we saw a large batch of Chinese and they did look odd. The majority – with their chests bare – wore multi-coloured suits; some wore peculiar-shaped straw hats and others wore prehistoric headgear. They were all more or less grinning and I presume just returning from digging as they were carrying all the necessary tools. Right opposite here the Canadian divisional sports will be held which are to last three days. We are preparing a place for the long jump, over 17 ft. At the place above where men were buried, French civilians were also buried. On some graves there were beautiful wreaths. I thought it was so touching. Saw a grave with some large wreaths and on the framework there was a square piece of looking glass and inside was a photo of the boy buried there; he was such a nice-looking fellow.

July 5th

Went to Ordinance today to bring away stores. Helping to erect a marquee on the sports ground. Met a fellow there from 37th Siege who I had not seen for eighteen months. I only recognised him by his voice as he had altered so much. He recognised me immediately. The Sergeant Major told us that if Fritz sent any balloon over today there would be a prize of five francs given to any man who took one of the dropped pamphlets to the Mayor at Duisans, but I did not see any.

July 6th

Sports start today. Watched them from 1 p.m. until 7 p.m. and it was very exciting. General Baron, Corps General, issued the prizes after which he gave a little speech. There was a Lieutenant Slaughter who won every race he entered – about six. A splendid runner. He was like a panther and took it so calmly and could cover the ground like a horse and yet never seemed to exert himself in the least. It was he who won the long jump with over 19 ft.

July 8th

My turn up the line again today. My time is spent continually making connections. Just now we are making a raid and have been observing it from the top of an old house. When it commenced it gave me a fright and I soon went to have a look.

My, it must be simply murder for Fritz; it's like one huge fire all along the trench. Can hear them whizzing over my head at a tremendous rate, salvos at a time. This lasted about twenty minutes. This afternoon I walked to our position at Artillery Valley and fired 5 rounds.

Left here at 2.30 p.m. and got back at 7. It is about seven miles walk. In a raid which we had last night, we had a few wounded but none killed. We blew up a dugout with over 80 men in it. They would not come out. No telephones are to be used any further forward than Arras. Being relieved today. Hear that we are going out on two weeks' rest.

July 12th

Paraded at 11 a.m. and walked to Haute-Avesnes, three kilometres distant. Sorted out five of our guns for handing over. Arrived back at 5 p.m.

July 13th

The usual 9 a.m. parade. Fritz's aeroplanes were over last night dropping bombs. They could be heard quite distinctly overhead and seemed to remain stationary. There were 12 or more dropped and some within a few hundred yards that shook the hut. Some of the boys in the next hut got up and walked about. Fritz has often been over here, but have not heard him for a week or two.

July 14th

Relieving another signaller at the exchange today. I was coming back from Tilloy Wood and nearly got caught. Fritz sent over a salvo, a three-gun battery, and without exaggeration they dropped not more than twenty yards away. I at once dropped down an old disused trench which was luckily nearby. Had just walked across the open for 500 yards. Again, fate was kind to me as in this trench there were some good dugouts. These shells were coming over three at a time with five-second intervals. No sooner had one lot dropped, another was on the way. In the intervals I was dodging from one dugout to another. On nearing home he stopped. The officer seemed anxious about my safety because we met in this open field, he going to the position and me returning.

July 15th

Went to centre position to bring away all our belongings. The detachment of Canadians who have relieved our party are the same men that we relieved nine weeks ago. I seem to have nothing to do now but eat, drink and sleep. Examined all lines for handing over.

July 17th

Very quiet today. Sir Douglas Haig is supposed to visit the 'flying ground' at the back of our billet. I borrowed Mr Starling's glasses and viewed the surrounding country from the top of an old house here and could see Douai fifteen kilometres away. Had a run on the bike to Arras to try and get some milk. This afternoon I did some washing. I had to take off my clothes and wait until they dried before I could put them on again. Fixed up a clothes line on the roof of an old house. The Canadians are trying our skill of firing at old bottles, which we stick up in the windows of an old house nearby. They are mad devils these fellows but good sportsmen. They talk to their officers just like old pals and even borrow money from them.

July 20th

The 17th Corps were relieved today by the Canadians at 9.30 a.m. After waiting about for an hour or so we rode in waggons to a village by the name of Ramecourt, two kilometres the other side of St Pol and thirty-eight kilometres from the place we left. On the road we met miles of transport, all Americans, who were going towards Arras. I am billeted in an old barn here. Just as I was making notes, about 9.30 a.m., the captain came round and complained at me having a naked light – a candle on a tin. He asked me if I had heard the orders regarding this and I told him I hadn't, as I had been for a ramble in the meantime.

July 21st

After the usual 9 a.m. parade I was dismissed. I then went on fatigue at the officers' mess and before I knew where I was I was marched away 'between two files' and taken in front of our captain, an altogether fresh part for me to play. Beside the captain there was the major and sergeant and a corporal. After writing out a crime sheet he asked me several questions on restrictions re lights etc, to which I pretended ignorance. The case was dismissed and I carried on with my fatigue. This makes it the second time our CO has tried to catch me. This man seems to be doing all he can to cause trouble amongst the men in this battery. There is a guard that has to be furnished at the barn and one at the General's *chateau* every day. This is our captain's way of smartening our ideas up but am afraid he will soon come to the conclusion that it does not pay. There were two men tried this morning and four others waiting, just for some paltry offence. Had a run as far as St Pol this evening and found a very nice place where one can have a good meal.

July 22nd

We are supposed to be on rest and yet are having three to four parades a day. This afternoon I visited the French open-air baths, only a stone's throw from where we are billeted. The deep end is 13 ft and the shallow end 3 ft. This bath is made of concrete and has four diving boards.

July 23rd

Physical drill from 7 to 8 a.m. Took 'A' section on telephone instruction until 10.30 a.m. Inspection of rifles and revolvers at 11.30, then finished for the day. Again at the baths and thoroughly enjoyed it. Shifting our quarters to another barn so as to be all together.

July 24th

Parades as yesterday. Took 'A' section in signalling instruction. Laid out a length of wire, connected each end to a telephone and sent each other messages. An officer was with the party. Finished at noon. At 6 p.m. I mounted guard here at the barn and finished at 6 p.m. the 25th.

July 26th

While in the baths the other day, who should come in but our captain and two others. They were speaking about organising a competition and asked me if the men would like it. I said I thought so and that we could muster up another twelve swimmers in the battery. I believe he is going to do his best. I just revel in this sort of exercise.

July 27th

The usual parades and on guard at 6 p.m. It is quite a regimental affair, mounting guard. Everyone stands around and is made an exhibition of and at times it causes a big attraction, which is rather embarrassing. Went to St Pol and did a little shopping and indulged in the usual meal.

July 28th

On guard outside the gates at the General's *chateau*. He has gone on leave and the Colonel is taking his place, therefore the guard has to be turned out for him. As I am writing, there is a jackdaw sitting only a foot away from my feet. He has been eating out of our hands and nothing seems to escape his sharp eyes. The bombardier was washing himself and this bird actually picked up the soap and ran away with it. The corporal did not know until I told him. It looked so funny seeing him run away with it in his mouth. It is now standing on one leg. Just going to do my second turn of sentry. I picked this jackdaw up in my hand and it appeared quite at home. It belongs to an ASC chap here. Have seen heaps of Americans and trainloads of tanks passing here daily, which makes me think there is a big thing ahead.

July 29th

Finished guard at 10 a.m. Going for a swim with No. 2 section.

This is a new idea and the CO is encouraging it. In the evening I went to a place in the village to get some eggs and chips. Had not been in many minutes before a fellow of ours came in and said we were to hurry back and pack up our things for the line once more. There was a big round-up because the order did not come through until everyone had gone out. Some had gone to St Pol. The military police at the bottom of the road had instructions to let no TMs pass that way. There were two or three chasing us on bicycles all over the place. Went to get my washing, which was still in the tub, so had to bring it away as it was. Kelly has got into trouble again. He stole a bicycle from a fellow and sold it to a Frenchman for 35 francs. The CO and this Frenchman came round the ranks at 11 p.m. with a torch to see if the culprit could be detected. When he found they were coming round like this he fell out of the rear rank and came back again after they had inspected everyone. Have just heard that when this bike was sold someone there knew his name was Kelly. Also after this he as good as owned up, which was the means of him stopping behind. Left Ramecourt at midnight and arrived at the Canadian camp near Maroeuil at 1.30 a.m. on the 30th. Turned in to bed and rose at 9.30 a.m. Had an inspection and was dismissed. No man is allowed to leave the billet. Two detachments were told to be in readiness to proceed up the line any time and on no account must they go away.

July 31st

Were allowed out providing we came back sober. Two men, including this man Kelly, came back drunk and could hardly stand up. They both stood outside the door of the mess and called the captain some shocking names. They wanted to fight him and made such a disturbance that every man in the battery was called out to put these two in the guard room, but the majority had gone. It was then decided that three men would be enough and I was one of them, but did not attempt it by force as one of these fellows was a boxer. Finally an officer, one who was well liked, just spoke quietly to them and they went away like lambs. The captain's brother, who was about the same in disposition, was travelling up here on a motorbike early last night when he collided with a lorry. He fell off his bike, got concussion and died shortly afterwards. It is said that he was scorching and had had a good drop to drink. Fritz's aeroplanes were over in large numbers last night and it was the biggest raid I have ever seen. They were bombing for hours and some came very near. One machine came quite low overhead and we could distinctly hear him cut his engine. Some were so frightened that they ran out and got into a trench nearby.

August 1st

Going up the line today. Relieved the Canadians. When our party arrived at Tilloy position they were just in time to see a premature that they had. Hardly a particle of the gun was left and two or three were wounded. It was at this place that we had the last accident. Went in a house on the Cambrai Road and commandeered a large looking glass, which I carried up and placed in the officers' den. It was 5 ft high by 2 ft wide. We have taken over a new position at Neuville St Vaast, about five kilometres to the right of Tilloy.

August 6th

Had a run on the bike to a village called Beaurains. Took off my clothes and washed them. Drying them only took three hours. There is a court martial coming off tomorrow for the two men who made the disturbance.

August 7th

Relieved today. Have to find the new billet. When I got to Anzin I enquired of the town mayor whether he could tell me where our battery was. He at once put me right and found out that I was only half a mile from home. Found this was at the old mill; some were billeted there and others in huts. It was a fine place for bathing.

The result of this case came off today and there was only one man convicted: the one who stole the bicycle is to be tried later. The other man's punishment was 90 days in the trenches. I think the captain was afraid of him and made it as light as possible. He said the man was so drunk that he did not know what he was talking about. Even after the verdict he said he would let him off after a month.

August 9th

Yesterday I was on guard. Visited a village today and heard that the King and Sir Douglas Haig were here and inspected the new 14.4 guns and the King was supposed to have put in the charge. There is a 12 in. howitzer nearby which makes a tremendous report. The shell of this new gun weighs 16 cwt =1,892 lbs and when fired breaks all the windows for miles around. The boys in the village could not sleep and were glad when it was shifted.

August 10th

Another fellow and I went up to the right sector and coming back had a look round Arras. Went in the old cathedral and museum. In this place I saw some huge pictures. Had a swim in the river at the back of the billet, which is said to be a tributary of the Scarpe. This afternoon a friend of mine had his washing attached to a line that was allowed to remain in the sluice gates where there is a continual rush of cold water, which apparently has a better effect on the clothes than soap. As it was being pulled in it got caught underneath, so I tucked up my trousers and walked along a plank that had fallen across the bed of the stream. After a little effort I fell in and got soaked so I came out, took all my things off and went in again and fortunately saved some of his washing. My foot felt as if I had a scratch on it and on looking I found one of my toes severed. Could not make it out as I felt no pain. I suppose it was the coldness of the water that accounted for it not bleeding. The doctor came to bandage it up and said I should have to go to hospital. It is quite a trouble to walk and took a long time to get to sleep with the pain. The boys were very good in bringing me anything I wanted. My foot, although well wrapped up and under the clothes, is icy cold.

August 12th

Saw the doctor this morning and left at 11.30 a.m. after keeping me for two hours. He seemed somewhat nervous and in pulling the bandage off my toe he opened the wound and made it bleed freely. I felt myself coming over faint so went out in the fresh air. Was taken by motor to the dressing station at St Katherine's. The major stitched my toe and I was then inoculated in the chest. I then had to sign a statement saying it was an accident and I also had to give names of witnesses to say they saw me in the water. I hung about here until 5.30 p.m. before I was taken to the Divisional rest station in Duisans. I am now in bed in my ward at 7 p.m. I had to have my toe inspected; this makes it the third time today that I have taken off the bandage. Was told that I would not be able to walk for weeks. I asked if I could remain at my battery and rest my foot but the doctor would not let me go as he said I might get lockjaw. There are a large number of artillery chaps here that have been gassed.

August 14th

Fritz was over last night and dropped five or six bombs in succession. Nearly all one side of this ward rushed out. It gave me a fright and my heart was in my mouth. The last one came so near that it threw up all the dirt onto our hut and the noise of that made us feel more frightened. Could hear the machine quite plainly overhead and wondered if the next was going to blow us to eternity. To make it more ghastly he even dropped lights to see what damage he had done. I prayed that he would not drop any more but he returned later and hovered over the huts again which made me think he was going to repeat the operation, but am glad to say he went away. Had another really good bath and a change and got into 'blues'.

August 15th

Again Fritz gave us a look up – always about 9 p.m. and dropped seven right off – about 600 yards away this time. He commenced sweeping with his long-range guns all round this place. Have the band playing outside this hut sometimes and a phonograph in the room so we are kept lively. There is an American in the next bed to me and you ought to hear him talk about what they are going to do: it puts years on one. There are two life guardsmen opposite me, and they are fine fellows, one is 6 ft 3 ins. tall and a splendid entertainer. Have had the stitches in my toe out this afternoon. Went to a concert this evening, a very good show. I noticed a large lump had made an appearance on my throat and I asked the doctor what it was and he said it was cyst. It was not serious and if it did not trouble me it is best not to undergo an operation. The 51st Scottish Division are taking over here now. They are very regimental with everything and so different to the last division. Each man is now issued with a ticket for his meals. They seem to be having a general clear out for the new division that is taking over and marking as many fit as possible. Hear a push is to be made on this sector and eight divisions of yanks are going over. This accounts for clearing the hospitals. Saw 38 of our planes up over here yesterday that I expect were going on a raid.

August 21st

A heavy bombardment woke me up this morning at 4 a.m. The doctor was round and marked out everyone except four, including myself. Jerry gave me an abrupt awakening about 1 a.m. this morning.

August 22nd

Was extremely warm today. Left here after dinner for another rest ration, with the 17th Corps, based 13 miles distant and about five kilometres from St Pol. This place is on exactly the same ground as the Trench Mortar school where I was last Xmas and it has now been turned into a hospital. This is well within shelling distance from the line and yet it is full of nurses. It is partly because the casualty clearing station (CSS) is attached. Sometimes we hear the groans of the men undergoing operations. There has been heavy shelling going on continually for four hours and it is still raging. The RAMC from the above rest station moved away so had to get our breakfast at the CCS. Have now been transferred to the 33rd CCS. It is now 5 p.m.; the bombardment is still on and has been for 24 hours. They are clearing everyone out to make room for the wounded. There are some Italian soldiers here. Some have been taken out for X-rays. A nurse, a very nice girl, dressed my foot. All nurses are in charge of these wards. Fritz was dropping bombs again and some patients got up. I hear that we brought down a large Gotha with five occupants, four killed and one wounded. Left here at 2 p.m. and rode in lorries to Ligny-St Flossel and then boarded a hospital train which was waiting there for us. Did not start until 6 p.m. and arrived at Etaples at 10 p.m. Had every attention in the train and the nurses came and spoke to us about the Aurora Borealis, etc. Motors were waiting at the station to take us to the hospital, which is a huge one and must hold 10,000 patients or more. My, what a treat to have a really good bath and get in between two nice clean sheets and being waited on hand and foot is just like a dream.

August 26th

Shifted today to another ward, which was the one I ought to have gone to at first, but it was full up at the time. They have mostly American nurses here. Went for a walk and attempted to climb one of the high hills but was prevented on account of some machine gunners firing. Instead I went to see the sisters playing croquet; all American ladies – you should hear their twang. I thought it rather nice so I played one of the girls there. She seemed to be a good player, beating all the others. We can see the sea from the door of our ward; it is only about a mile away and nine miles from Boulogne.

August 28th

Watched a game of baseball last night between the Yanks and Canadians, which was very exciting. The former were the Chicago Boys, which was written across their jerseys. They were fellows of fine physique. The latter beat the former. They are very clever at the game and it is amusing to hear the remarks passed between the two teams, as they get very enthusiastic. There were American nurses there who were just as excited as the boys. This afternoon I walked to the top of one of the hills, which I think was about 1,000 ft high. You get a splendid view of the surroundings with the sea all around us and it seems as if you are on an island. This is the place that was bombed out twelve months ago. Fritz came down low and machine-gunned the nurses – supposed to be well over 1,000 killed. If Jerry is expected overhead, the bed patients are put in the dugouts nearby.

August 29th

There were about 15 of us in this ward marked for Blighty. One fellow has a little cut on his finger and another a small sore on his foot. In fact more than a few said to me that they don't know why they were being sent back to England, as there was nothing the matter with them. Some are surprised that I have not gone, as my case is much worse than some of theirs. A gas case in the next bed said he was only 'shamming', and that when he'd been really bad he'd been turned away as all right. Out of the twenty men who are going, there are only about six genuine cases. There were four men, including myself, marked for a convalescent camp today. We left at 1.30 p.m. and arrived at this camp at 2.30, only a few miles away. Went through the usual routine. Saw the doctor etc. This is a champion place for sport, with everything under the sun; it is a huge YMCA. You can go to school and a dancing mistress even teaches dancing. If any man wishes to take up boxing he is likely to remain here for two months.

August 30th

About 700 of us paraded this morning and were marched down to the beach about three miles away. Had the band with us, which caused a bit of excitement when passing the various hospitals. We got to the beach and had an hour of rugby. Then for an hour we had dancing to the accompaniment of the band. Had our boots, socks, hats and coats off. Packed up at 11.30 a.m. and marched home again. There is a beautiful resort three miles away called Paris-Plage, where Jack Johnson used to train. Was at a concert tonight and the brass band were there which made the evening very enjoyable.

August 31st

We were inspected by the Colonel this morning. Was again at the concert tonight and it was a splendid show. Paraded before the MO. Again, a lot were sent to another convalescent camp at Trouville.

September 2nd

Yesterday I was on fatigue at the cookhouse. Some of the boys are being taught dancing in the YMCA. There was a big dance held in the concert hall this evening. WAACs were there with their partners. I watched for a good while and found it very enjoyable.

September 3rd

Have been selected for the tug-o-war team. Were practicing with another team and won every time. Went to a concert this evening, which was very good, Lena Ashwell's party. I was taken off the team and told to stand by for going away tonight. Sports here today. There were WAACs, VADs and Sisters. The latter pulled against the WAACs and won. They were much bigger girls; the former are only about 5 ft 2 in. tall.

September 6th

Had breakfast at 6.30 a.m. and drove to the trains at Etaples. Started off at 7.45 and arrived in Boulogne two hours later. We left in cars for the convalescent camp at Wimereux, about four miles away. Went to the baths, the finest I have ever been in, with steam and shower. In the evening I saw a boxing match.

September 8th

Yesterday we went to church. Today visited Boulogne. Walked all the way – six kilometres and the wind so strong that it almost lifted us off our feet. We arrived there at 4 p.m. Went in the soldiers' home where we were waited on by a bevy of pretty girls. Had a walk round the town and watched some leave boats coming in and arrived home at 9.30 p.m. It rained the best part of the way home.

September 9th

My legs were so stiff this morning that I could hardly walk. It tells on one after a month or more in hospital.

September 10th

Got up at 5.30 a.m. and left at 7.30 for another hospital about a mile distant. Were on fatigues carrying sandbags and making the huts splinter-proof. There were a large number of German prisoners working here. Finished and landed home at 1 p.m. Went to a dance in the evening.

September 11th

Left here at 8 a.m. for fatigue at another hospital in this neighbourhood. Had dinner there and left at 3.30 p.m. Went to the town of Wimereux about one mile distant, which is a nice little seaside resort. It boasts a very large casino, which has been turned into a hospital.

September 13th

Yesterday paraded at 8.30 a.m. We were all marched to the top of a very high hill. We were given an hour's exercise and the band gave us a little music. Saw a boxing tournament in the evening.

September 14th

Looked up Boulogne again. Got a train from the town here all the way and the journey took just an hour. It rained the whole evening and in spite of the weather I had a fairly good time. Coming home in the tram I got into conversation with one of the WAACs and she was telling me how they fare. They have a rough time of it. They have the same food as we do, get punished for quite small offences and have to delegate duty the same as us. There are sports at Wimereux today. Jim Driscoll, Bandsman Rice, etc. are boxing. Was inspected by the CO for the last time.

September 17th

Left Wimereux today in buses for St Martin's camp in Boulogne. They have a fine system here. There is a large blackboard that stands on the square with the times of departure of all parties and where they are bound for, so each man knows all his particulars. The meals are all very good; the cooks are women and they are extremely clean. Each man is issued with a ticket that has to be given up before he can have anything to eat, therefore putting a stop to double meals. The WAACs serve the meals and they are well cooked, better even, I think, than I had in hospital. Had a run to Boulogne this evening – only twenty minutes walk from here.

September 18th

Leaving here at 12.30 p.m. for a train in the town. Train left at 2.50 p.m. and arrived in Etaples at 4.45. Stopped for one and a half hours and found ourselves at Abbeville at 9 p.m.

September 19th

Got to Rouen at 6 a.m. and after an hour here for refreshments etc, we entrained and three hours later landed at our destination in Honfleur after a total train journey of nineteen hours.

Walked to our camp and after the usual red tape were allotted to certain tents. Paraded at 2 p.m. and was served out with deficiencies in kit. Went to one of the many picture shows here and thoroughly enjoyed it. Wrote to the captain to ask him if he would claim me back.

September 20th

Paraded at 8 a.m. and listened to the camp orders being read out. At 9 a.m. I saw the doctor to be inoculated. Have to have all our hair cropped close, although a large number do not like the idea. On account of inoculation I am excused all duties for 48 hours.

September 21st

Was on parade at 5.30 a.m. This is usually the one for warning drafts. Met one of our signallers who is assistant cook and has been here a good time. He left our battery two months ago. Paraded at 7 a.m. for the gas chambers, to test our respirators' resistance to tear and cloud gas. Before leaving for the line, everyone is given a new gas respirator and has to have it tested by the above method.

September 23rd

At 5.30 a.m. we were marched to Honfleur Station, six miles from Le Havre to load up waggons for two camps and then returned to ours and unloaded. In the afternoon we were carrying rations from a store to the cookhouse and it was very hard work.

September 24th

Was on fatigue in one of the dining halls, taking dinners to the different tables and washing up the numerous dishes. They have a rack that holds well over 2,000 plates and there are over 600 mugs. Did not finish until 5.30 p.m. One of the corporals is there. He left the battery three months ago and I am leaving here with him tomorrow. A young fellow of 20 is leaving here for Woolwich to pass a test to become a staff sergeant. On fatigue at the officers' quarters.

September 27th

Paraded at 8 a.m. and were all inspected by the Major and dismissed. Again we made an appearance at 3.30 p.m. in full marching order and after an hour of waiting we left with the band at 4.30 for a six-mile tramp to Le Havre station. Entrained and left at 9 p.m. after waiting in the train for an hour or two.

September 28th

Landed at Doullens at 11.30 a.m. after waiting for three hours. Arrived at Achiet-le-Grand at 7.30 p.m. after 22 hours in the train. Marched to reinforcement camp nearby. We slept in a tent, 14 altogether. Fritz was over but did no damage about here. Fritz occupied this camp only five weeks ago. According to the state of the ground and the old trenches I should think it was quite true. The nearest part of the line is said to be 20 kilometres from here, which proves that the enemy was pushed back a long way. There are two parades a day at 9 a.m. and 2 p.m. but I attended neither. Another fellow and I had a ramble round the old trenches and saw a large number of enemy shells and Trench Mortar bombs. Further, we came across one of our aeroplane bombs that had been dropped when the enemy held this ground. It weighed about 80 lbs, had wings and resembled a pear in shape. Saw a very badly damaged armoured car and one of Fritz's *Minnenwerfer* positions and ammunition. In the evening I walked to the railhead and saw some damaged tanks, including whippets, being unloaded and then put on trucks specially constructed to carry 40 tons. The latter are said to be able to travel 15 miles per hour. The captured enemy guns, when Jerry evacuated this village, are all being guarded and are just here by the station; some are very large. The Church Army hut is an enemy marquee and a fine one it is; different altogether from ours and has quite a dozen proper windows with hot ventilation holes. The only one of its kind I have ever seen and far superior to ours.

September 30th

Went for a walk this morning and did not have any parade. In the evening a companion and myself walked to Bapaume, six and a half kilometres distant, arriving at 7 p.m. On account of having to get back quickly we did not have much time to have a good look round. I should think this town is about the same size as Ypres.

October 1st

Commenced at 9 a.m. filling up shell holes, which took about an hour. In the evening, after purchasing a few eatables at the canteen, I went into one of Fritz's dugouts, lit a fire and enjoyed our snack of pears and cake, the latter broken and mixed with the pear juice. Just after I came out of the canteen, Sir Douglas Haig's car pulled up outside and he alighted and walked along the road past our camp.

October 2nd

Our corporal and myself were told to pack up. After hanging about the station for two hours we entrained and left at 12.45 p.m. arriving at Bapaume thirty minutes later where we cooked ourselves a meal. Had a look round and saw some of the enemy's tanks. This town is badly damaged. Left here at 2.30 with a full pack and carrying two days rations; also new boots. Marched to a village, or what remains of Morchies, ten kilometres from the place we left. This is supposed to be the 17th Corps reception camp but is nothing more than three or four dirty old stables and not fit for pigs to sleep in. It is so dark that we could barely see each other. One of these stables was six inches thick with manure and had to be cleaned before the men could lay on the floor. Anyway, I had a look round and saw an old French cart and cleared out all the old bricks in it, borrowed a large tarpaulin from the quarter stores and the corporal and I had a comparatively clean and dry bed to sleep in.

October 3rd

We departed from here at 2.30 p.m. Walked to the main road two miles distant. Got a lift on a lorry for six kilometres along the Cambrai Road, then got out and made enquiries about our headquarters where we arrived at 5.30 p.m. Slept in a tent with three more of our battery signallers. Can see Bourlon Wood, it is only about 1,000 yards away and ten kilometres from Cambrai, the church spire of which can easily be seen. Left here at 8 a.m. for our battery, which is just below Morchies and arrived there at 11 a.m. After a good dinner we were shown to our quarters, an old German dugout. Could not sleep because of the noise of the guns. On the road we passed the Canal du Nord, which was completely dry. A large bridge that had been at this spot was utterly destroyed and lay in the bed of the canal. There are some gigantic holes or craters along this part of the main road caused by the enemy's mines during his retreat: the idea being to impede our progress.

October 5th

Did a small job taking a hut down and loading it on a lorry. The village in which our battery is situated, is called Lécluse. A quantity of four loaded waggons left for a village called Paillencourt about nine kilometres distant. Worked until 7 p.m. carrying stores to our quarters that consisted of old German dugouts. The waggons pulled up as near as they could to the quarters, as they were on high ground well above the road, hence the carrying of these stores. The hardest day's work I have done for months.

October 7th

Yesterday I was busy rigging up bivouacs and unloading some of the previous day's goods. Having a rest today so walked to Bourlon Wood, about an hour's tramp. Looked around this place for souvenirs but found nothing more than an old German paper. Nothing but a mass of fallen trees and shell holes here. Was paid out today, the first in the battery for over three months. These papers *Leipziger Neueste Nachrichten* and *Tremonia* are dated 8th and 9th September 1918 respectively, about two weeks previous to Jerry evacuating. There are a large number of troops passing along the road making towards the trenches. A bombardment opened out about 8 p.m., which I presume were gas shells and kept on for hours.

October 8th

Was told to report to Captain Towler of the Signal Service at corps headquarters about a mile away. A violent shelling opened out at 4.15 a.m. and was the commencement of a fresh stunt. Am now settled with the Signals and in a tent with the other signallers of our battery. Had an offer to take over as servant to above officer but did not accept it. When I reported for duty here there seemed no one to take any notice so with another fellow, Ennals, we walked to a large village called Fontaine, near Cambrai. In the afternoon, loaded up a couple of lorries and went with one to the advanced signal post beyond above town. Passed the villages of Cantaing-sur-Escaut, Fontaine and Proville and went round the suburbs as Cambrai was on fire at the time and no traffic was allowed to enter. After two hours run we got to our destination at 6.30 p.m., the forward advanced exchange. It seems terrible to see this fine city burning. It has been like it for days: before the enemy left, this is what he did. There are three or four very high churches, the spires of which can be distinguished for ten miles. We captured this two days ago. I saw heaps of mutilated horses lying on the road and some were gashed about terribly. Considering there were very few dead men, just one or two here and there, the ground seemed to be in a fairly good condition. The reason for this is because Fritz did not show fight. He was absolutely beaten and we gave him no time to consolidate by keeping him on the run. All the bridges across the Scheldt Canal were destroyed.

October 10th

Arrived home last night at 9 p.m. Slept very little all night with the noise. Jerry was over bombing for hours. A very big attack started at 4 a.m. All day loading up waggons with stores prior to moving off. The report this morning is that Fritz has retired so far that we have lost all trace of him for the time being, but our cavalry is still keeping him on the run. Have shifted from our tent, four of us, to a dugout nearby, as the former is too dangerous at present. Everyone has gone from here now except our little party. The guns have been going hard all day. Our observation balloons have shifted up to beyond Cambrai. The rations have just arrived and I am the duty cook for today. We had a very enjoyable dinner, the largest since Xmas 1916, fit for a horse. Had a hunt round and found an old pail in which I cooked the cabbage and potatoes. I fried the beans in about a quarter of a pound of butter and finished up with a good drop of tea. I peeled the spuds and cut up the meat with an old razor. As a rule the cook has no appetite so gave half of mine to the other boys, which they thoroughly enjoyed. Have never before cooked a cabbage. This afternoon I walked to where our battery was and got some cigarettes and I noticed numerous buses passing along the main road full of troops going towards Cambrai. I counted over 20 in a few minutes and it appears they have been passing for over an hour.

October 12th

Had to pack up our things, load up a few stores and left at about 10.30 a.m. Arrived at a village six miles in front of Cambrai by the name of Cauroir. After unpacking the lorry we proceeded further and landed at another destination, Avesnes-les-Aubert, a rather large and modern village that is four miles beyond the former one. There are two or three rather large casinos here and one is said to have been built by the enemy for the pleasure of his men. Have heard that the best of the ladies here were frequently made to entertain the Boche in these places and by their past actions I do not disbelieve it. Another fellow and I are in a very comfortable room in a cottage, which has a fine civilian bed and a nice stove. There are fields upon fields of vegetables about, which the enemy evidently meant to use themselves, so there is nothing much we miss in that way. There are also two nice lamps in this room that are very handy. Am writing by one at the present moment. Have just got back, 9 p.m., from running out one and half miles of wire. We had to join onto another line that army headquarters had run halfway between their place and this. This is the advanced exchange and as some of the infantry make headway so we have to follow and keep up the communication. Extremely heavy shelling again this morning.

October 13th

The advance exchange is shifting again this morning. Every other day we seem to be making a move. This is exactly what I like, plenty of adventure. The Heavy Artillery headquarters is taking our place. The room where we are billeted even had pictures on the wall, left just as it had been before the people had to run. Have to take my turn on the exchange, two hours on and four off. We have two boards to operate and one is cordless. There is a Morse code operator at my side, dummy key, when he gets a message I have to transmit it to nearly twelve different units and headquarters and visa versa.

October 14th

Came off above job at dinner time. Saw one of Fritz's aeroplanes bring down one of our balloons only just outside this place. He dived from a good height and dropped an incendiary bomb on it. Nearly every night when it is dark this balloon goes up ready for the morning observation. Have shifted the exchange about twelve miles away to a *chateau* near the station. There were very few messages coming through after midnight. The exchange here is in a cellar and is like an office, it even has a typewriter. The people who had this place before are shifting out so we shall have it all to ourselves. Had a walk round here today and found an old crucifix on one of the houses, which I commandeered. Also, in the same place I saw a lot of German magazines on the table. It is well to see that Fritz has held this place for a considerable time, as all the streets are German named. This village, or small town, is damaged very little and the enemy has held it since 1914. There is Boche writing everywhere. Each house has been allotted for so many of his men and has it written outside each house. The French people who are here, are few, and have never seen British Tommies before and on first seeing us were very surprised. Especially since they were told that the British were losing and all manner of lies. Some French people were down a cellar and when our people first took over and were called upon to come up, exclaimed, 'English, English, soldiers *trés bon*'.

Just had a message through while on the exchange that when the French captured Laon two days ago they found 12,000 civilians and they put up another balloon in the place of the one that was burnt. Have to walk from our billet to headquarters exchange for our meals, nearly a mile. Had a fine tasty meal of cabbages, potatoes and bully; our supper is the most enjoyable meal of the day.

October 17th

Just a year ago today since I went on leave. Heard that yesterday we took the village of Haussy, five miles away but Fritz counter-attacked and took it back again. We got about 1,010 civilians from this village and as many prisoners. The former are at present in the town hall, and some are pitiful sights: women with babies in arms, crying with joy who seem as if they can hardly contain themselves. Saw two of our inhabitants here, who appeared quite cheery and said good morning to us. It seems rather strange to see civilians after only just taking the place over. The first I have seen for a long time. Our authorities have posted up notices to the effect that we must not damage French property. So by that it seems that we are certain that Jerry will not advance again, hence the civvies will soon be settling down.

October 18th

Did an hour's fatigue outside headquarters. When we went to draw our tea from the cookhouse we saw one of the REs amongst them dressed up in a top hat, white shirt and collar, black coat, vest and striped trousers, and a large and conspicuous red bow; also a stick under his arm. He looked so out of place yet very comical mixed up with all the ruffians. He was waiting in a queue with his tea bowl under his other arm. He walked down the main street with his mug of tea in one hand and flourishing his stick with the other, and everyone roared at him.

We all had a fit of sneezing. Fritz has been sending over some new gas. We have now got bombs weighing one ton, which stand 11½ feet high and cannot be dropped at an altitude lower than 8,000 ft because of the terrific explosion and maelstrom which can result.

October 19th

One of Fritz's exchange switchboards is being used here and like all things it is very original. Our infantry went over at dawn and the bombardment opened out at 2 a.m. Have to leave here at 1.30 for the next advanced position. The civvies tell us that before we took this town they were forced to walk in front of the enemy's guns, both women and children. Arrived at this new place, St Aubert, 5 kilometres away. The mud and slosh about here is awful, mostly due to the continual flow of traffic going towards the line. There were only two NCOs and myself to unload a lorry of signalling stores and in doing so a chap knocked an airline pole in my eye and at the time the pain was excruciating. What with that, the pouring rain, and ankle deep in mud and no place where I could rest quickly, I felt more fed up than ever I have been before. I was absolutely helpless: could do nothing. I was as blind as a bat and felt I hadn't a friend in the world. What with the noise of the never-ending stream of vehicles and the whizzing of shells overhead, I thought at the time I should go crazy. The worst of it was that I was left by the two NCOs in a dirty little room, the floor covered with mud and hardly sufficient shelter from the concussion of a shell, let alone a small one landing on the roof. This was at 9 p.m. and I was all on my own until breakfast the following day. They said they were afraid to stop here all night and went to find a more suitable shelter. I was not afraid but felt terribly lonely and I shall never forget that night. If Fritz had concentrated his fire in the same area as I was in I don't think I could have budged. Fritz was shelling intermittently all night which was not very comforting, especially under the circumstances.

October 21st

After a most horrible night I reported sick in the morning. I was told to go back for all my belongings as I would be going down the line. I arrived at the main dressing station near Cambrai at 3.30 p.m. There were also wounded civvies there. After having tea I left for the CCS near Bapaume. After getting into bed thinking we would be settled for the night we were called out to go further. I landed at another CCS a few miles the other side of Bapaume.

October 22nd

I was in two different wards at the above place. Left here at 4 p.m. and entrained but did not move off until 8.30 p.m. We finally arrived at Abbeville after a 13-hour run to No. 1 South African general hospital. The staff are all South African and there are three eye cases altogether. We sat in the front seat of a car, which was driven by a VAD nurse, the hospital being about two miles out of the town. After a good bath I got right into bed. At the above station they had the aid of German prisoners to lift the stretchers from the train to the cars.

October 25th

The doctor here seems a very considerate man. The Sister in this ward has a military medal and the Matron has quite a string of decorations; she must have at least half a dozen including a Victoria Cross from the Boer War.

October 26th

Still in bed but believe I have to get up tomorrow. A convoy of wounded have come in today from the line. The nurses say that there is to be a big evacuation for Blighty today. Had the bandage taken off my eye and replaced by a shade. All in the next ward are going to England, but only one from here.

October 28th

Got up today, the first time for six days. There is a Paddy in the next bed to me who told the nurse that his clothes were walking away from him so the nurse got her torch and had a look. She soon found there was some truth in what he said and he was given a change. She threw the dirty ones on the floor and was told to walk to the other end of the ward and call them.

October 29th

The nurse came round early this morning and told us that Austria had thrown in. The doctor came round, examined my eye and said, 'I see you belong to the RGA. You can be marked out.' On the way to this hospital, at the time we passed over the Scheldt Canal and through Cambrai, I saw a lot of civilians carrying their little bits of odds and ends. I felt so sorry for them although they were overjoyed at their deliverance.

October 31st

Yesterday I drew all my belongings out of stores, made up deficiencies and today I am off again. Left at 8.30 a.m. in a nice bus with glass all round. Every seat is inside: even the driver's and the engine keeps it very warm here. Passed through the town of

St Valery and going up by a cemetery we saw some fifty French women who had been attending the graves of their loved ones. Arrived at Cayeux at 12 noon. We immediately had dinner and were put in tents. This is a convalescent camp and a seaside resort, quiet but very bracing. This is an extremely large camp and there are supposed to be between 8,000 and 9,000 troops here. There are twelve or more large refreshment huts and a picture palace. I have seen some large dining halls but this one is huge and can seat nearly 4,000.

November 1st

There is a seaside resort near here called Brighton to where I sometimes walk but it is very lonely. There is an eighteen-year-old American in this tent from northern Pennsylvania, a nice quiet boy reminds me something of Joe. He was saying that it took him 14 days to get to France. A lot of these fellows are well spoken and seem to have come from good stock. Walked to Brighton and all the large houses are used as cafés. I went into one, a *chateau*, and had eggs and chips. The coffee was as good as I have ever tasted. There was a piano and we had a singsong, which made it very enjoyable.

November 7th

For the last two days we have had continual rain and no parades. Have passed the time away reading. Was on physical training this morning, the first parade since my arrival here.

There was a tremendous row here this evening: it is thought the war is over – the cheering was terrific. Seemed as if there were thousands of voices. The band was playing, whistles were going and lights were being sent up. This is supposed to be the Armistice. Everyone appears to be going mad. The canteen – expeditionary – was raided and the damage estimated at £300. In the town the French were giving away free drinks. The Colonel gave us a lecture about looting and told us what would happen if there was a repetition.

November 11th

On fatigue at the quartermaster's stores. Last night I saw the picture *David Copperfield*, it was very good. We were told that a telegram is to be read out to the troops between 9.00 a.m. and 2.00 p.m., a confirmation of the Armistice and were told to control our excitement. Have just come off parade and heard the peace terms read out by the Colonel. It was quite an auspicious occasion. We are given a complete holiday for 48 hours. There is a list of sports and entertainments prepared for us and everything is free. We are allowed to go anywhere in France, no passes are required so long as we get back at the end of the given time. An effigy of Fritz is going to be burnt tonight on the square. A short church service for all denominations is to be given in celebration of the victory.

November 12th

The bonfire was still alight at breakfast time. Last night the band marched up and down the square playing popular airs. French civilians were allowed to come in and share our joy. Some were dancing in front of this fire that was giving out a great heat. The *Marseillaise* was played and French boys were held up shoulder high. There must have been thousands round this fire. When the guy finally fell in the furnace there went up a great roar. Free concerts were given in all the huts.

November 14th

It is extremely cold here and so healthy that I should like to live here always, even if it was only a 'But and Ben'. I never felt more healthy in my life – hence happiness. Went for a long walk all along by the sea for about four miles. It was exceptionally cold to start but when I returned my blood was all of a tingle. There is a tower on the beach, which was used by the coast guards for observing. I climbed up the tower but could not see far as it was too foggy. The tide goes out for nearly a mile and the stretch of sand is very extensive, just like a desert. I met an old *padre* leisurely walking along and reading a book and he nodded to us; these fellows are very sociable. Had a walk to Brighton and a

Canadian and myself walked out to meet the sea. We were watching the tide gradually coming in. We were there for no more than two minutes and upon looking back I found that in the meantime the tide had surrounded us. We had apparently been standing on high ground. Had no time to waste thinking about it as the longer it was left the deeper it got so took off my boots and socks and to my surprise the water came up to my knees. The other fellow walked through it without removing his boots.

They have classes here to improve one's knowledge and get one prepared for a trade or profession in civilian life.

November 17th

Yesterday I went to Cayeux for a few hours in the evening. Did not go to church today, Sunday. Instead I went for a walk to a small fishing village by the name of le Hourdel, an hour's walk from our camp and six and a half kilometres from Cayeux. Went to a small café and had coffee and cognac but did not think much of the latter: it was very sickly. This is like a small harbour and the end of the land. Could not go any further forward so had to do an about turn. All in all I was out about 2½ hours.

November 18th

Was on the CO's inspection this morning and marked fit for duty. Visited the pictures this evening and saw two splendid pictures, one was called *Human Bloodhound*.

November 20th

Did not parade yesterday but had a walk along the beach to Cayeux and quite enjoyed it. There were 900 of us on parade inspected by the Colonel. All for evacuation. Some of the houses at above place are very unique.

November 21st

Paraded at 3 p.m. for Honfleur. After walking to the station we entrained and left at 6 p.m. arriving at Noyelles later that night. On the way we passed over the mouth of the Somme. Waited in a canteen on the station for 3 hours and arrived at our destination at 2.30 p.m. the next day. After 14 hours journey we alighted at Rouen where I purchased some views of the city. Were put in the old tents again. Visited the pictures and then wrote to the captain of our battery to claim myself back, as before.

November 23rd

Was on clothing and medical inspection and getting clothes out of store, occupying all the morning. Paraded again at 1.30 p.m. with all my kit and was transferred to another camp. Had a walk as far as the Australian camp, a mile distant.

November 24th

Was on officers' mess fatigue this morning at 6.40. Finished at 2.30 p.m. Each man was given a large piece of bread pudding and it was delicious. Hear that Gunner Moir is here and running this 'Housie' school and has been doing so for twelve months.

November 25th

Went to the 'pimple' to go through gas again, both sorts. I volunteered for an escort to go to Southampton to take some German prisoners. I got all ready in marching order, including three blankets and rifle and bayonet and hung about with all that load from 3 p.m. until 5 p.m. Then there was a roll call and there were about twelve men not required, including me, so I took the opportunity and bunked off in case the Sergeant Major changed his mind. To make it worse it rained the whole time. Was quite a relief to get off this job. Afterwards I had a walk to the city centre, four miles off.

November 26th

Have followed the example of others and had a walk round so as to dodge all these unnecessary parades, half of which are only red tape. I met a Mons fellow here who was in the same tent as me at the reception camp at Achiet-le-Grand and we are going about together here. He went up to the Sergeant Major at above place and tried to get in my battery by altering the regiment in his pay book 15th Trench Mortar battery and telling him he had been in it since 1915. But it was all in vain and they could not help him. He was told that this ought to have been dealt with at the Honfleur RCA depot.

November 27th

A draft has just arrived from Blighty. They have only had four months training and three of them have been put in the same tent as me. There are a large number of men continually going up the line from here. A battalion of the Guards has left for Cologne. There was a riot in these towns (the two RGA camps), through having too many parades and a shortage of rations. They gave them one loaf for 14 men. They demanded more but were refused so they broke all the windows in the dining hall, but this ration was made up the following day. The other camp started the same thing but was given the extra loaf at once. The parades have been shortened, our pay has been doubled and the passes to Le Havre doubled. The Colonel gave a speech on the subject and was booed and hooted. All seemingly dislike him. He has been at this depot since the war started. That is his punishment as he is said to be the instigator of the Lipton Meat Scandal.

November 30th

Was on the 6.30 a.m. parade, not 5.30 and the second one since my arrival. I was chosen for armed picket, which would operate in the event of a riot. All were given rifles and ammunition. We do nothing but answer our name, twice a day. The draft that left here for Cologne I saw confirmed in the paper today.

December 1st

One thousand men are leaving here today, including myself. Paraded at 2 p.m. all ready to go but it was cancelled.

December 2nd

It was posted up in orders that all men that have been over 13 months without leave have to give in their name at once, which I did. When I got back to my camp I was told that I had been wanted for a draft that had already gone but in the meantime my name had fortunately been crossed off owing to leave. I had to see the Sergeant Major and explain where I had been and he said that my leave made no difference. If I was down for draft I would have to go. Two or three times drafts are being cancelled – even marching away with full kit, then returning an hour or two later. They do not seem to know what to do with us. One party paraded on three separate occasions and took their rations for the long run and each time they returned and had to hand in everything.

December 3rd

Went on parade and expected to have my name called out to go away but to my surprise it was not on the list, so took it that my name had been taken off for leave. Nearly all the men here are surprised to think that they are still being sent up the line. One party got ready to leave at 1.30, with rations and hot tea being served. Then they were cancelled, as there were no trains available.

December 4th

The names of all miners are being taken. The first to be de-mobilised. Saw a fine picture here last night *A Romany Lass*, which was in six parts.

December 5th

Have to report to No. 12 camp for leave. Left at 9.45 a.m. to walk to Le Havre station. Entrained at noon and left 40 minutes later, arriving Rouen at 4.30 p.m. Walked through the town to another station. We left at 6.20 arriving Boulogne at 6.30 the following morning.

December 6th

Stopped at rest house near the quay. Left here at 1 p.m., embarked at 2.30 and landed at Folkestone one and a half hours later, finally arriving Victoria at 7.45 p.m.

December 21st

Leave over. I left home at 4.45 a.m. and had to walk to Victoria Station. Entrained at 6.30 arriving Folkestone at 9 a.m. and Boulogne at noon. Marched to St Martin's camp.

December 23rd

Was at above camp for over a day. Entrained and found ourselves at Rouen at noon. Walked about two miles through the town to another station. Entrained at 6.30 and left three hours later, landing at destination four hours hence. With two other companions we indulged in a good meal at Honfleur before going to camp. I was a day late in returning and had to report at the orderly room. After explaining my case to the clerk he told me to 'get off' so I was lucky as some had seven days for being one day late. I met an old signaller here who I had not seen since I left Pembroke Dock on September 16th.

December 25th

Had a really good Xmas dinner. There were entertainments galore. In fact about the best and merriest time I have had in my life. Was invited to the Aussies' camp where I was well entertained and went to their pantomime and returned to above where I did good justice to my tea. In the evening we went to one of the concerts and a dance where each was given a little souvenir and heaps of other things.

December 26th

Went to a good concert and a pantomime where there were a few WAACs taking part. It was a very good show. There was a parade at 8.30 a.m. but I was missing. Had been pouring all day with that very fine rain which soon gets one soaked.

December 29th

The last two days I have been going to concerts, pictures, etc. In fact, leading quite a bohemian life. Paraded for the line at 10 a.m. but did not leave for another two hours. Left Le Havre at 4 p.m., arriving Etaples at 9 a.m. the following day.

December 30th

We were put in tents for a few hours and at 1.30 left for Lille, where we arrived at 3.30 p.m. the next day.

December 31st

Walked to billet, four miles distance. This is a fine city with very large buildings and some that would put our London ones in the shade. Were billeted in a high school and in a huge room that contains 48 large windows. It would be ideal for a great ball, being about 100 ft long by 30 ft wide.

Final Days, 1919

January 1st

Paraded at 11 a.m. and was dismissed. Visited the city and had a good look round. Coming home we got quite lost and it being so dark made matters worse. Instead of entering the Porte de Roubaix we came through Porte St Andrew, which took us in the opposite direction to the town and the way we had to go. We crossed the La Basse Canal and nearly fell in as it was so dark. In fact we were attempting to get over a bridge which was an awful mass of ruins. There was not a soul to be seen and we might as well have been stranded in a thick forest. However, after finding our way to the station at St Andrew we made enquiries of the RTO and he directed us. We had to retrace our steps again and go in an altogether different direction. We were beginning to give up all hope but eventually we got back quite safely. Food is terribly dear here. Mince pies, which used to be 2d, are two francs each, approximately 1s. 5d. A French civilian saw us looking in the window and said in good English, 'They are very expensive aren't they?' It sounded rather odd coming from him.

January 2nd

Took some mail bags to the APO in the town. Went to the Gaiety Theatre. What a huge mass of masonry there is and enough surplus room to build another theatre. There are five circles and a large promenade on each. There were a lot of French people here as well as Tommies. It was a Blighty company, 'Bert Errol'. The lady impersonator was amongst the company. Had a run to Roubaix this afternoon by train, about 11 miles; it took 45 minutes and we arrived there at 4 p.m. Visited the casino, which is turned into a picture palace with French and English patrons and is elaborately lit. Arrived back at Lille at 8 p.m. and before leaving had a good supper. There were still large German posters all over the town of Roubaix, giving instructions to the inhabitants. One can buy large coloured bills showing the awful treatment towards the people during the enemy occupation.

January 3rd

Were put on an hour's fatigue cleaning up guns. Had a good look round Lille for the last time. On nearly every street one can see small crowds singing the French 'Victory Song' and there were many women without a dry eye. It is such a catchy tune and everyone seems to know it, even the small children. I bought the words from a man who was singing it at a street corner. Our letters are no longer being censored.

January 4th

Leaving Lille for the 3rd Corps. Arrived at St Saviour station at 1 p.m. and had to return on account of no trains running. Went to a concert that was very good. Met an old officer of our battery, Mr Pearce, who is now in the Flying Corps.

January 5th

Left here at the same time as yesterday and hung about until 7 p.m. before entraining. There was hardly any shelter from the pouring rain and all about the station was thick with mud. After seven hours journey we arrived at Halle, 16 kilometres from Brussels at 2 p.m. the following day.

January 6th

Went to 3rd Corps. There was a rest camp where I stopped until dinner time. Enquired of RTO where we had to go for our respective brigades and were then directed to a village called Lembeek on the Mons Road. We found that the 70th Brigade headquarters was at a place 4 kilometres distant. We landed here at 4 p.m. and were posted to 157th Siege battery near the headquarters. Whilst waiting at Lille station I visited a café. There was a baby there whose father was a Boche, even the neighbours' children seemed to know. We were billeted in a school room with a cosy fire and it was very comfortable.

January 7th

Paraded at 9.30 a.m. in a field. Because of the new arrivals we had to shift our quarters to a bakery on the main road, about half a mile from the battery. We had to go to and fro three times a day for our meals and carry them through the village in our hands and they were often cold before we arrived. Had to pack up again and go to another battery in the same village. Sent to one billet in No. 6 Section and afterwards shifted to another with No. 4 Section.

January 10th

For the last few days there has been nothing much doing. Have a very easy time with just the 9 a.m. parade each day. Left billet at 7 a.m. for Brussels, where I arrived an hour later. Had a bath in a French place, then went to the YMCA. This is a gorgeous building. It has a large German store, is illuminated most magnificently, has three or four large lifts and every convenience imaginable. Had some photographs taken.

January 11th

Arrived back at billet in Saintes at 9 a.m., just in time for parade. Went to a whist drive in the evening that was held in a school. I nearly won a prize. I had to cut the cards between three of us and it happened that we had four each time; cut again and I lost.

January 14th

Yesterday I went to a lecture about the remodelling of the map of Europe.

I am doing a little washing today. There is an old man in our billet, 89 years old. He is a bachelor and lives in this place all on his own. He is wonderfully strong and exceptionally active for his age and has an abnormal appetite. Sometimes he will sit for hours with his old pipe, quite contented and hardly attempting to move.

He'll sit round the fire all the time as he feels the cold. We've grown very fond of him and he often gets little bits given to him. I believe he is well connected, as there are some rather nice people who always visit him on Sundays. I can always remember this old man as he consistently shouted 'Fermez la porte!' – shut the door.

January 15th

Visited Brussels by myself. Caught the 7 a.m. train and had a good look round the town and inside the town hall. Saw the ballroom that the Duke of Wellington danced in before going to Waterloo. This place is supposed to contain the most beautiful staircase in the world. Landed home at 9.30 p.m. Have put in for a four-day pass to Antwerp.

January 18th

Left here at 4 p.m. for Brussels. Went with guide to view the places of interest. Visited the skating rink and enjoyed the run immensely. There were some very fine young skaters there. Arrived home at 9.30 p.m. the following day.

January 20th

On guard in the village for 24 hours; my first for nearly six months. It is a very easy one, as I just have to ensure that no one runs away with the guns.

January 25th

Had to go before the Colonel this morning about my pass to Antwerp. He said he would have to see the General, which I did not believe. Wanted to know who I was going to stay with and if they were quite all right, etc. He even asked why I wanted to go to this place and seemed to make quite a fuss about my few days' holiday.

January 26th

There is a march past today at Brussels before King Albert. Anyone can go and the idea is to review our troops.

January 28th

Was looking forward to a trip to Louvain yesterday but it was cancelled. Saw the Colonel again about my pass. He said he had got it through.

January 29th

Went to a lecture on travel cinematography. Enquired at Brigade headquarters about my pass, as I ought to have had it by now. I went round three times between 5 p.m. and 9 p.m. Went to Brussels this afternoon. Accompanied a touring party and explored the summit of the Law Courts. It is a gigantic edifice and cost ten million dollars to build. The top, or dome, was said to be too heavy for the foundations and had to be reconstructed. The architect is said to have been so severely criticised that he committed suicide. To get to the top we had to climb 540 steps and only a few were allowed up at a time. I think this is the largest building I have ever seen. The large dome is gilded and on a fine day it can be seen for 20 miles. It stands on very high ground – the highest point of the city. It is said to be a masterpiece and the largest monument in the world. The big hall alone is 3,600 square metres. The building commands this part of the town and is 90 metres high.

January 30th

I got my pass at 8 a.m. Left billet at 9 a.m. and arrived in Brussels at 11 a.m. I was too late to go to Antwerp so had another day in the capital. Saw the interior of the museum and stock exchange. There was a fire in a street at the back of the YMCA. The occupants in the top story were calmly throwing their furniture and belongings out of the window. The firemen climbed onto the blazing roof and sprayed it with their hose; but some of it had already fallen in. It was a very risky job and the roof was at an angle of about 72 degrees. I went to the skating rink, which was very gay, and watched them play a game of golf.

January 31st

Left above by the 9 a.m. train and landed at Antwerp two and a half hours later. Had dinner at a large German hotel, which is temporarily used as a Belgian YMCA. Quite an aristocratic place. A lift took me to my quarters, which have every convenience. Had a good dinner and booked a nice bedroom. Went to see the town Mayor who was in this very large building; which originally were the offices of a large diamond merchant. While waiting, a Frenchman took me in the lift to the very top of this house and introduced me to a pretty mademoiselle who was cutting diamonds. In the evening I went to a music hall, which I enjoyed. It is rather amusing as one can walk into any part of the building without interference. I was in the circle to start with and after the interval took a seat in the stalls. There was a fine tableau at the last and they sang the 'Victory Song'. It was a three and a half hour show. After coming out about midnight an Aussie and myself found, on going to our rooms, that there were others sleeping in our beds so we had to try and find another place to sleep for the night. Luckily we got a suitable place not far away. It was a really good bed and after we had finished talking to the landlord it was past 1 a.m.

February 1st

Had a look round the skating rink, which is rather a swanky place. You pay as you go in and are charged for a seat. Visited the cathedral that was built between the years 1047 and 1226. It contains a unique and magnificent pulpit. A marvel of sculpture and oakwood representing Adam and Eve driven out of the terrestrial paradise. The pulpit was placed there in 1776.

February 2nd

Leaving here by the 8.40 a.m. train, arriving Brussels at 10.30 a.m. Had a splendid swim in the baths here and it was worth the ten shillings. There was mixed bathing and plenty of sport. I had a good shower and there were little cubicles of hot water for washing one's feet. This is all included for one shilling. Climbed to the top of the Congress Column, 45 metres high. Saw the Law Courts again and went to the rink.

February 3rd

Leaving today at 10.30 a.m. for billet. Whilst at Antwerp I went to see the cathedral, which is supposed to have the sweetest chimes of any church in the world. It is 123 metres high and before the top is reached one has to climb well over 600 steps. Walked to the Grand Square in Brussels and left there in a lorry for Saintes, arriving at midnight.

February 4th

Hear that while I have been away I missed two chances of being demobilised. On guard today. Saw the orderly about my ankle, which has swollen to the size of an egg. I asked him if he could give me some lint as I wanted to attend to this myself, as I feel sure that if the doctor saw it he would send me to hospital. I am told that it is septic poisoning. Signed the necessary forms for going away.

February 6th

Leaving for home today. Arrived at the village of Enghien at 10.30, 8 kilometres distant and was billeted in a hut. My foot is very painful and so swollen that I am almost frightened of the results. Before I left I had to be relieved of guard duty as the pain was excruciating and after walking up and down with these heavy boots on it now seems worse than ever. As it happens, I am having a good deal of tramping to do and I dare not report sick with it now and am praying that it will not get any worse. I do envy the other boys who are able to walk anywhere. I am a fixture. What with the snow on the ground and bad circulation, my feet feel like blocks of ice.

February 7th

Left about 9 a.m. and marched 4 kilometres to Enghien where there was one of our own trains, an L & South West, waiting for us. It looked so out of place there. We departed at 11 a.m. and arrived at Dunkirk at 9.30 p.m. the next day.

February 8th

The train journey was 35 hours and the cold was intense. Hear that one man succumbed on the way. We had a good bath and a clean change, which was very acceptable.

February 10th

The rations we get here are starvation rations and it is quite a common thing to wait an hour before we can fight our way to get a bite to eat. It is much worse than trying to get into a theatre on a bank holiday. In fact I have bought my tea out many a time.

February 11th

Reveille at 4 a.m. Marched 4 kilometres to the docks. Embarked and left at 8.30 a.m., arriving at Dover 3 hours later. Marched to a camp near Fort Burgoyne; my first place on joining up. It all seemed so familiar. After a lot of humbugging about I left the station at 8.30 p.m., arriving at my final destination of Victoria at 11.30. Thought it too late to go home so got a bed and a meal at the Church Army.

February 12th

Landed home just in time for another breakfast.

The Great War was officially over on 31 August 1921 when all Treaties of Peace had been ratified by the respective governments.

- 10 January 1920 – Ratification of Treaty.
- 8 March 1921 – Further allied advance into Germany through non-compliance with our terms.

August 31st 1921

- Total killed on all sides – thirty million.

- Total cost – £4,000,000,000

- The first bomb was dropped in Britain on 24 December 1914 at Dover. It weighed 22 lbs and no one was killed.

- During the War forty-eight airship and fifty-nine aeroplane raids were made on this country, thirty-two of which were on London. 4,820 civilians, soldiers and sailors were killed and injured and more than half that number were women and children. Monetary damage caused amounted to £3,000,000

- Total enlistment from August 1914 – November 1918 – 8,819,896

- Personnel – 14 August 1914 – 733,514

- Total killed in action, lost and died from wounds – 908,375

- Grand total of men enlisted in the Army, Navy, and Air Force to November 1919 – 9,669,311*

- Grand total who died for the Empire – 947,105

[This information was obtained by my father at the time from newspapers and other sources, and is accurate as written in his diary.]

---

* NB: Prior to 1918 there was no 'Airforce' as such. The RAF was formed from an amalgamation of the Royal Naval Air Service and the Royal Flying Corps.

Extract from a contemporary newspaper listing:

THE CHIEF WAR DEBTS (in round figures)

Owing to Great Britain by:

France	£623,000,000
Italy	£533,000,000
Jugo-Slavia	£28,000,000
Rumania	£25,000,000
Greece	£23,000,000
Portugal	£22,000,000
Russia	£722,000,000

With smaller amounts from other countries making a total of £1,981,000,000

Owing by Great Britain to America:
£915,000,000

(Which is being repaid with interest at the rate of £33,000,000 a year, to go on till 1984 when over £2,000,000,000 will have been paid – principal and interest)

Owing by France to:

Great Britain	£623,000,000
America	£797,000,000

Note on the Author

STUART CHAPMAN was born in 1888 in Portpatrick, Scotland and was one of four boys. The family returned to England in the early 1900s where their mother started a business which later became a large and well-respected firm of wholesale grocers. During the First World War, Stuart's eldest brother managed the business while his three brothers were away.

After the War, Stuart joined the family firm together with his brothers, who all survived their war years, but he found it difficult to settle down. He always had a sense of adventure and loved to travel. He toured the UK and Europe and, in 1928, left England on the SS *Montroyal* for Canada, with a view to taking up farming there. He lived on farms in Alberta, Saskatchewan and Manitoba for over a year, working very hard and enjoying the experiences, but realised that farming was not for him and came home to England.

He returned to the family business for a year or so, then left to open a business of his own. He married in 1931 and had three children. In 1943, during the Second World War, his business was destroyed by a bomb hitting a railway line nearby. He survived and then joined the Civil Service, where he stayed until he retired in 1956. He died in 1967.

He always had a sense of adventure. He was very strong, physically, but also a deep thinker and a sensitive and quiet man. He loved art and reading, particularly biographies, and I still treasure the watercolours he painted in the 1920s and early 1930s.

Margaret Chapman

Glossary of abbreviations

APO	Army Post Office
ASC	Army Service Corps
CCS	Casualty Clearing Station
DAC	Divisional Ammunition Column
DSO	Distinguished Service Order
HAG	Heavy Artillery Group – term used in 1915–1917
HGA	Headquarters Garrison Artillery
HE	High Explosives
HLI	Highland Light Infantry
KOSB	King's Own Scottish Borderers
MO	Medical Officer
NAS	Naval Air Service (RNAS – Royal NAS in full.
NCO	Non Commissioned Officer
OC	Officer Commanding
OP	Observation Post
OR	Other Ranks (as opposed to officers)
RA★	Royal Artillery
RAMC	Royal Army Medical Corps
RE	Royal Engineers
RFA	Royal Field Artillery
RGA	Royal Garrison Artillery
RMF	Royal Munster Fusiliers
RTO	Railway Transport Office/Officer
TF	Territorial Force
TM	Trench Mortar

| *VADs* | Voluntary Aid Detachment (Nurses) |
| *WAACs* | Women's Auxiliary Army Corps |

* From 1899 to 1924 the Royal Artillery was split into Royal Field Artillery (including the Royal Horse Artillery), which manned the field guns supporting the infantry and cavalry, and the Royal Garrison Artillery, which manned the heavy and siege guns. The term Royal Artillery was still used in a generic sense to describe the RA and RGA.

1241954R0

Printed in Great Britain by
Amazon.co.uk, Ltd.,
Marston Gate.